Simplified Essentials:

Graduate Counseling Supervisions and Skills My Professors Forgot to Teach Me

Camelia Shaheed, Ph.D., LPC, CRC
Department of Disability and Psychoeducational Studies, The University of Arizona

innovativeink
PUBLISHING
A Division of Kendall Hunt

Cover images Shutterstock.com

innovativeink PUBLISHING
A Division of Kendall Hunt

www.innovativeinkpublishing.com
Send all inquiries to:
4050 Westmark Drive
Dubuque, IA 52004-1840

Print ISBN: 979-8-3851-8632-7
Ebook ISBN: 979-8-3851-8633-4

Published in the United States of America

To all the Counseling Skills & Techniques students who taught me
And to three who taught and inspired me
Clarissa Pflug
Kevin Vincent
Paige Willer

Beware the need to protect and be protected
Each erodes freedom

CONTENTS

FOREWORD

This book evolved out of necessity. Finding a text that "fit" graduate student needs, my needs, and CACREP criteria was a challenge. So much to teach, so many handouts ignored. Without question, counseling or therapy and supervision are complex. They take deep dives into what makes people tic. Life is messy, but here's what I hope is one straightforward and convenient package that shouldn't strain clock or wallet. No fluff and I struck a deal with the publisher to keep cost low. Alert me of errors. I'm rushing to have this for class in August.

My students describe me as direct, tough, and fair. This book reflects that description. Neither perfect nor sexy, it provides experiential material. My hope is it promotes client welfare, not glorify us. Most of all, it's for anyone whose illusions need to be replaced with something concrete. What I mean is -- if you expect political correctness, get your money back. Fresh out, plenty of respect and experience to share.

I'm shameless when it comes to clients. To ensure the best care possible, a clinic would save time and increase competence as students transfer knowledge into service. We need money. Elissa exhaustively canvases our community for clinical settings that must be regularly assessed for appropriateness. Why a clinic? Positive outcomes are predicated on consistency. As a student, I received excellent supervision from professionals unafraid to push without killing my creativity. Then, as now, I relied on two Hollywood characters – see inside on Columbo and Callahan -- who personify key clinical traits. One, help clients gather data without locking horns. Two, speak little while doing it. I mention this because we need strong clinicians. If you have dollars to spare on growing minds, help us promote the hope business. THANK YOU.

CS

The University of Arizona camysmarvel@arizona.edu.

HOUSE-KEEPING

Reputation is a byproduct
of action, not words

I applaud your strength to dig deeper into your past. First, you have a tailored safety plan. Second, as we go deeper, some things may or may not occur. As a gardener, you know things emerge when you disturb the soil – worms, bugs, fungi, bottle caps. Similarly, clients sometimes report new experiences -- disturbed sleep and dreams or being more emotional. Disturbing as they may be at first, we can use those experiences in this work.

Notice my word choice throughout. Hope cannot recede into the background. Clients, from the first visit that covers the therapeutic informed consent (TIC), know change is hard and has a cost. I must communicate about risk while I maintain hope. Yes, there can be consequences, but we can use them to our advantage. Incidentally, this process helps clients maintain enthusiasm for therapy and the clinicians for the profession. It also helps maintain healthy boundaries to reduce, if not avoid, burn-out and vicarious trauma.

Before we leave this section, note the skills in **Open** below, skills of a typical first session. The rest is part of the first and subsequent sessions. Unlike the movies in its continuous and strategic attention and intention.

SKILL: STRATEGIC & INTENTIONAL	EXAMPLE or INSTRUCTOR COMMENT	SKILL TIME STAMP	DID IT OR NOT
Open	**(TIC Obligation: Each session: Do you want to kill or hurt yourself and/or someone else?)**		
NO READING			😊 ☹
Listen to client language ID clt's personality style Plan to avoid treatment concerns related to that style	In/Dependent, oppositional, aggressive, assertive, passive From the start, kindly redirect, clinical self-disclose or provide FB from the start.		😊 ☹
ID clt's communication style Your plan to avoid treatment concerns related to that style	Quiet, talkative/pressured, philosophical, concrete From the start, kindly redirect, clinical self-disclose or provide FB from the start. Caution re quiet clients and the trap you're likely to fall into		😊 ☹
Be alert to the state of ambivalence or little/no motivation	==		😊 ☹

SKILL: STRATEGIC & INTENTIONAL	EXAMPLE or INSTRUCTOR COMMENT	SKILL TIME STAMP	DID IT OR NOT
Specify session agenda that *IDs primary concern – a behavior*			😊 ☹
Housekeep: Start of session: Non-therapeutic FB per TIC			😊 ☹
Reiterate "feelings", "change", "redirection"			😊 ☹
Risk assessment			😊 ☹
Clt summarizes last session's key work IF clt missed key item > ADDRESS	**Clients summarize because:** **1. We know change is more likely when we hear our-selves talking about it or aspects of it** **2. Focus remains on client, not us or how well we re-member the session** **3. Alerts us re client inner workings and what "stuck" this session and the next session when the client be-gins with a summary of this session.**		😊 ☹
Homework review: If you don't review, won't get done			😊 ☹
Influence			
Rapport			😊 ☹
Silence (mandatory, but will make contextual sense)			😊 ☹
Redirect (always to avoid bad habits)			😊 ☹
Reframe			😊 ☹
Feedback			😊 ☹
Clinical, not personal, self-disclosure			😊 ☹
Personal resources as indicated			😊 ☹
Cognitive-emotive balance sheet of change consequences			😊 ☹
Link clt verbal and non-verbal			😊 ☹
Reflect content (L, M, H): **2 max, regardless of type**	Use as much as you like during ambivalence. Other-wise, it kills rapport.		😊 ☹

SKILL: STRATEGIC & INTENTIONAL	EXAMPLE or INSTRUCTOR COMMENT	SKILL TIME STAMP	DID IT OR NOT
Reflect Affect (L, M, H), **2 max, regardless of type**	Use as much as you like during ambivalence. Otherwise, it kills rapport.		😊 ☹️
Pace/timing			😊 ☹️
Challenge: mixed messages, discrepancy, ambivalence			😊 ☹️
Brief, NOT session, summary, links **Primary** emotion to content			😊 ☹️
Re-story (goals, personal resources, cog-emot balance may change)			😊 ☹️
Action			😊 ☹️
ID, educate, practice, "teach me", do			😊 ☹️
Throughout			
Comportment, affect, tone, pace, language, physical/verbal tics			😊 ☹️
Encouragers, not serial reflections (use your face, body, sounds, 1 word)			😊 ☹️
"I" statement redirection			😊 ☹️
Spoke briefly, to the point, no long explanations			😊 ☹️
NO advice, unless client is truly stuck. If so, advice addresses both sides of the issue			😊 ☹️
NO rescuing			😊 ☹️
NO power struggles, judgment			😊 ☹️
NO leading or advice			😊 ☹️
NO interruptions			😊 ☹️
NO "WHY?"			😊 ☹️
NO "BUT"- negates clt or what was said directly prior			😊 ☹️
Focus on designated concerns OR discuss avoidance of them			😊 ☹️
LIMIT/convert questions to statements (passivity, attorney/witness, false agreement) Concise Open Questions for data or clarity, Closed are strategic and rare			😊 ☹️

SKILL: STRATEGIC & INTENTIONAL	EXAMPLE or INSTRUCTOR COMMENT	SKILL TIME STAMP	DID IT OR NOT
Close/End			
Future pacing			😊 ☹
Clt summarizes session --- Do something if clt misses a point	**Clients summarize because:** **1.Change is more likely when we hear ourselves talking about it or aspects of it** **2.Focus remains on client, not us or how well we re-member the session** **3.Alerts us re client inner workings and what "stuck" this session and the next session when the client be-gins with a summary of this session.**		😊 ☹
Reorient clt to positive (turn off "live" wires). Rewards…			😊 ☹
End session/Conclude treatment			😊 ☹
Instructor/Supervisor			
Min 55 minutes, max 60 minutes			😊 ☹
Setting: neutral and clean			😊 ☹
Professional attire			😊 ☹
Skills 😊 ☹ self-eval			😊 ☹
Skills DEEP narrative +/- self-eval (minimum 200 words, linking full term; concrete plan for each limitation)			😊 ☹
Skill time stamp			😊 ☹
Recording visual and audio clarity			😊 ☹

2

STATE LICENSURE & NATIONAL CERTIFICATION

To begin with differences between various mental health professionals, whose scope of practice can differ between states.

SPECFIC TASK	PROFESSIONIAL
Evaluation for Medication	**Psychiatrist** -Medical school graduate -Service: Trained to evaluate mental health via clinical evaluation for the purpose of medication. May deliver therapeutic services based on setting and specific role hired for. -License: State board medical doctor
	Psychiatric NP - MS nursing or doctor of nursing practice (DNP) -Service: Trained to evaluate mental health via clinical evaluation for the purpose of medication. May work independently or in collaboration with MD, depending on state. -Certification: Psychiatric mental health nurse practitioner

SPECFIC TASK	PROFESSIONIAL
	Psychiatric PA - MS in physician assistant studies (MSPAS) -Service: Trained to evaluate mental health via clinical evaluation for the purpose of medication. State determines whether work independently or in collaboration with MD. -Certification: Physician assistant-certified (PA-C)
Assessment & Therapy	**Psychologist** -Ph.D. or Psy.D. in psychology -Service: Trained to evaluate mental health via clinical assessment and evaluation, psychometric tools, all therapeutic services. -License: State board clinical psychologist -Some states allow psychologists to prescribe if they meet strict education requirements
	Clinical Rehabilitation Counselor (ClRC) -MA/MS in counseling or closely related field -Service: Trained in case management, advocacy, social justice. Encapsulates the scope of duties within clinical mental health counseling and more. Trained to work with clients with disabilities or chronic medical and mental health conditions, some psychometric tool use, all therapeutic services to behavioral change that can aid medication prescribed by psychiatrist, psychiatric NP, psychiatric PA. -Needs served: mental health, developmental disabilities, physical disability, vocational rehabilitation -License: State board LAC/LPC -Certification: National CRC
	Counselor, Clinical Mental Health Counselor -MA/MS in mental health: LAC/LPC, LMFT, LCADAC -Service: Trained in case management, advocacy, social justice; evaluate mental health via clinical assessment and evaluation; some psychometric tool use; all therapeutic services to behavioral change that can aid medication prescribed by psychiatrist, psychiatric NP, psychiatric PA. -License: State board

SPECFIC TASK	PROFESSIONIAL
	Clinical Social Worker -MSW: LCSW → LICSW -Service: Trained to evaluate mental health via clinical assessment and evaluation, some psychometric tool use, all therapeutic services to behavioral change that can aid medication prescribed by psychiatrist, psychiatric NP, psychiatric PA. -Trained in case management, advocacy, social justice. -License: State board

Licenses and certifications have subtle differences. Licensure is the legal, often state-driven, requirement to work in certain professions while certification, often national, typically documents skill in a profession. In counseling for example, licensure is represented by each state's independent licensed Professional Counselor while certification can be represented by the national Certified Rehabilitation Counselor certification. Here, I'll discuss the Arizona LAC/LPC and the national Certified Rehabilitation Counselor (CRC).

Licensed Associate & Licensed Professional Counselor (LAC/LPC; https://www.azbbhe.us/)

Please visit the Arizona Board of Behavioral Health Examiners (ABBHE) website for the most up-to-date information on

1. qualification for the LAC will precede the LPC
2. the necessary degree and coursework
3. the requirements to transition from LAC status to LPC
4. the necessary supervision required to qualify for the LPC
5. When the clock starts and stops ticking on your ability to apply for the LAC

Also, keep all graduate syllabi and clean records. When a problem arises, the board will require all documentation related to coursework, fieldwork, and possibly more. It can be excruciating, although I've found licensure staff helpful. Please note that licensure staff must adhere to the law, not to who we are or our credentials. Again, check that ego at the door, if only temporarily.

Never take someone else's word about anything that impacts your work or reputation. If you do, you're courting trouble. Verify everything. It is each applicant's responsibility to read and understand the requirements and obligations of this certification. I've seen the sad business that comes from missed opportunities when an applicant accepts someone's advice without verification. It is unwise to base your understanding of facts on second-hand information when you sign your name to it. After securing the license, the holder completes a designated number of continuing education units in designated categories to maintain it. The same applies to those who wish to participate in the Supervisor Registry.

Individuals who pass the CRCE needn't take the National Counselor Examination (NCE) to qualify for the LAC. The domains of the NCE fully align with Council for Accreditation of Counseling and Related Educational Programs (CACREP) requirements:

1. Professional counseling orientation and ethical practice
2. Social and cultural diversity
3. Human growth and development
4. Career development
5. Counseling and helping relationships
6. Group counseling and group work
7. Assessment and testing
8. Research and program evaluation

Such individuals will complete the Licensed Associate Counselor (LAC) application supplied by the state board and pay the required fee. After the individual meets the strict guidelines for hours and type of supervision from an appropriately-credentialled supervisor, the individual can complete the LPC application and pay the required fee. To maintain the LAC or LPC, the holder will complete a designated number of continuing education units in designated categories.

Certified Rehabilitation Counselor Certification (CRC; https://crccertification.com/)

Please visit the Arizona Board of Behavioral Health Examiners (ABBHE) website for more complete up-to-date information. It is each person's professional obligation to read and understand the requirements and obligations of this certification. It is unwise to base your understanding of facts on others, especially when you sign your name to it.

CRC is earned via an examination across 12 domains:

1. Professional orientation and ethical practice
2. Counseling theories, techniques, and evidence-based practices
3. Medical and psychosocial aspects of chronic illness and disability
4. Group and family counseling
5. Crisis and trauma counseling and interventions
6. Assessment/Evaluation, occupational analysis, service implementation
7. Career development
8. Case management
9. Health care and disability management
10. Business engagement
11. Community resources and partnerships
12. Research, methodology, and performance management

Individuals who pass the CRC examination (CRCE) do not need to sit for the state licensure CPCE. Such individuals will complete the Licensed Associate Counselor (LAC) application and pay the required fee. After the individual completes the required minimum hours, in their required designations, the individual can complete the required LPC supervised hours, complete the LPC application, and pay the required fee. To maintain the certification, the holder will complete a designated number of continuing education units in designated categories.

3

TREATMENT SETTINGS & LEVELS OF CARE

To understand the tensions and politics behind counseling, first understand community versus private services as well as levels of care.

Community-focused or public healthcare attempts to make healthcare more equal and accessible. That is, ensure that everyone receives care, even if they don't have insurance or can't privately pay. In comparison, **private healthcare** is a typically private practice where the provider accepts insurance or out-of-pocket payments instead of public health insurance Medicare or Medicaid. Keep in mind that private practitioners are increasingly accepting Medicare and Medicaid, which means public health dominates state or federal government funded services. Public health services are typically offered on a sliding scale, meaning clients pay what they can afford or nothing at all.

The primary benefits of community-focused services are access and cost. Some states are challenged with respect to treatment access. Rural communities, even with remote services, have built-in barriers to adequate care since public transportation is typically absent and owning a car is even more unlikely. Reduced or no service cost is the biggest benefit of public services. Public health care organizations, particularly those who subscribe to a true integrated care model, accept Medicaid and Medicare within a one-stop facility. They provide uncensored quality services to their communities.

One distinct difference between community-focused and private healthcare settings is the work behind the scenes. Publicly funded agencies have no shortage of clients while private agencies depend more on word of mouth, website display, and other factors for clients. That difference translates into a different work ethic. A private practitioner will work longer and "stranger" hours than the public practitioner. The private practitioner responds to all callers as quickly as possible. Often, that means evening work since the day is preoccupied with clients. The private practitioner will also worry about the cleanliness of the bathroom and availability of toilet paper, unless the practitioner's budget can tolerate additional staff for those tasks. So, much that's taken for granted in community-based clinics cannot be taken for granted in private clinics. Keep that in mind when, as a student, you want a field experience in a private setting. Expect evening texts from your supervisor.

Levels of Care

When a person seeks services, it's vital to provide the least restrictive level of care (LOC) possible. LOC refers to a range of available psychiatric services that vary in intensity, frequency, and duration. It's important to note that someone seeking assistance may be aware of only the obvious LOCs - outpatient and inpatient. Informed consent requires meaningful information, from the start, to save resources and time. Understanding the range of services is integral to positive outcomes. For example, simple bereavement is best addressed in outpatient care, not a partial hospitalization program. A partial hospitalization setting is out of proportion with simple bereavement. Client-clinician rapport and collaboration are integral to the management of self-stigma, perceived stigma, and guilt about mental health issues, which can be exacerbated by the provision of the wrong LOC.

In addition to determining the appropriate level of care for a patient, it is also essential to continue to assess throughout treatment to determine whether a patient would benefit from a higher level of care or may benefit from additional outpatient services such as group therapy or a twelve-step program. Communication is vital in helping patients feel confident and cared for on their road to recovery.

PRIMARY LOC	DESCRIBED
Level of Care (LOC)	Based on acuity level and what is considered best practice for that level, not on the client's lifestyle or other psychosocial factors. One LOC is differentiated from another by milieu, intensity, duration, and goals. **Golden rule: Always the least restrictive LOC.**
Inpatient Hospitalization (IP) Highest or most restrictive LOC	Monitored 24/7. For those who are actively suicidal, homicidal, or experiencing an acute exacerbation of symptoms that poses a safety risk to self or others. IP ensures safety and stabilization. For this reason, the unit is secure. Average length of stay is brief, 3 -7 days. Longer stays are based on safety needs and acuity of clinical presentation.
Residential Treatment	Well-monitored, but much less restrictive than IP with a milieu with a strong sense of community. These programs average 30-90 days based on the condition. Clients can expect to participate in individual and group therapies and receive psychiatric care. Differences from IP: setting and personalized treatment goals addressed in an atmosphere that relies on therapeutic community, often includes family members/supports, focused on self-awareness, self-regulatory skills, and interpersonal skills.
Partial Hospitalization Program (PHP)	Contrary to its name, this a more intense "outpatient" experience where length of stay depends on the continued psychiatric need for this level. To ensure this, PHPs undergo strict quality assurance and Medicare/Medicaid audits where payment can be denied. PHP typically occurs after IP or residential treatment. Clients receive primarily group therapy five days/week, six hours a day. They also receive individual therapy, weekly status reviews, and continuous medication management.
Intensive Outpatient Treatment (IOP)	3-5 days of individual and group therapies for three (3) hours/day up to 8-12 weeks (length of stay depends on client needs). A flexible structure that accommodates clients who work, attend school, or care for children.
Outpatient Treatment (OP) Lowest or least restrictive LOC	Community services – state/federally funded or private - for individual (50 minutes), group therapy (1.5 hours), and medication management. This level can be increased to accommodate client needs and mitigate a higher level of care.

4

SERVICES & BILLING

Billing occurs at multiple levels for clients since it depends on the service provided and at which level that service can be billed. Some services can only be billed at the case management or paraprofessional level. Some services can only be billed by specific professionals. For example, case management interventions can be provided by anyone below and including professional levels: care managers (CM) and practitioners at the MA/MS level. Therapy can be provided by anyone state licensed to provide therapeutic services: LAC/LPC, substance dependence, LMFT, LISW, RN, psychologist, psychiatrist, nurse practitioner, physician's assistant. The table below reflects who can provide what at the community mental health service level.

SERVICE	CM	LAC LPC	SA/SD	LMFT	LISW	RN	PhD	MD NP PA
Behavioral Health Promotion	Y	Y	Y	Y	Y	N	Y	N
Skills Training & Development Living Skills	Y	Y	Y	Y	Y	N	Y	N

Case Management	Y	Y	Y	Y	Y	N	Y	N
Psychoeducation Group	Y	Y	Y	Y	Y	N	Y	N
Therapies	N	Y	Y	Y	Y	N	If hired to	N
Psychiatric Eval	N	N	N	N	N	N	N	Y
Medication Eval	N	N	N	N	N	N	N	Y
Medication Monitoring	N	N	N	N	N	Y	N	N

SA/SD = Substance abuse/dependence

SERVICE	DEFINED	NOTE
Behavioral Health Promotion	Case management intervention. ***Taught*** client treatment planning to increase knowledge, attitude, behavior. Educated/trained utilizing a flyer [paste web link] to increase behavioral knowledge of the nature of illness, relapse and symptom management, med management, stress management, safe sex practices, HIV education, parenting skills education, and healthy lifestyle, diet, exercise. Note that community mental health agencies will require the specific language. Some insurance carriers in private practice may do the same if they pay for case management at all. No note? IT NEVER HAPPENED. Your word has no legal or clinical value.	CANNOT be billed as therapy, anyone excluding RN, MD, NP, PA can provide this
Skills Training & Development Living Skills Training	Case management intervention. Individually or group context, ***taught*** client independent living, social, and communication skills to enhance client's ability to live, participate in the community, and to function independently [choose from >]: Self-care, household management, social decorum, same/opposite-sex friendships, avoidance of exploitation, budgeting, recreation, development of social support networks and use of community resources. Note that community mental health agencies will require this specific language. Some insurance carriers in private practice may do the same if they pay for case management at all. No note? IT NEVER HAPPENED. Your word has no legal or clinical value.	CANNOT be billed as therapy, anyone excluding RN, MD, NP, PA can provide this

SERVICE	DEFINED	NOTE
Case Management	Basic non-professional intervention. These are neither therapeutic nor skills training services. This category includes all client and client-related contacts – telephonic, email, text - with client supports, other professionals who provide services, regardless of length. How you bill depends on the setting. In public and private practice, although considered a cost of doing business, it will be documented. In community mental health, it is a cost of doing business that's "captured" in the billing system per **Billing** below and documented regardless of length.	CANNOT be billed as therapy, anyone excluding RN, MD, NP, PA can provide this. LEGAL matter. No note? Never happened. Your word is insufficient
Psycho-educational Group	Case management intervention. Ideal for dispensing information about or education on behavioral or mental health concerns, especially to make informed decisions surrounding treatment. Often, these groups are precursors to more in-depth treatment. This service is valuable since it enhances therapies and natural supports by fortifying commitment from everyone involved. It also aids supports in understanding and learning "best fit" interventions to assist the client. Topics: specific conditions, medications, interventions that can enhance or minimize medication action, life and relationship skills. In many cases, these groups are pre-requisite to therapy, especially when clients need time for medication to become bioavailable before formal therapy. When a client and supports understand, they can cope better with ups and downs of treatment from the client's and their own perspectives.	CANNOT be billed as therapy, anyone excluding RN, MD, NP, PA can provide this. RN, MD, NP, PA can conduct a medication or diagnosis-related group.

SERVICE	DEFINED	NOTE
Therapies - **1:1, couples, family, substance use, group** (not psychoeducational group, which can be delivered by anyone)	Professional clinical intervention	Delivered by an independently licensed practitioner or someone under the supervision of an independently licensed practitioner (LAC, student-in-training)
Billing	***All client and client-related contacts, consults, messages, telephone calls, texts, and emails are documented *regardless of ability to bill.***** *To bill, activity will occur WITH CLIENT unless it's a support service like psychoeducation for client's supports or case mgmt. -Billing occurs in 15-minute increments with client or someone else if case mgmt *Less than 7.5 minutes: no bill but do document *7.5+ minutes but less than 15 minutes: bill for 15 minutes and document ***EX 1**: worked with client for 5 minutes – do not bill, but do document* ***EX 2**: worked with client for 8 minutes – bill and document* ***EX 3**: worked with client 23 minutes – bill for 30 minutes and document* ***EX 4**: worked with client 35 minutes – bill for 15 minutes and document*	Legal and ethical matters. Improper billing can lead to loss of license / certification to practice, arrest for fraud and/or embezzlement

5

SMART DOCUMENTATION

First and foremost, each document in a chart is a legal document. Never say anything in it that you don't want to answer for later. It's also an ethical document. The tone and word choices says more about you than the client. The client can behave as any client may – anxious, agitated, or impulsive to name a few. The practitioner, on the other hand, is held to a high standard. So, if you're frustrated, in a bad mood, tired, or generally feeling miserable seek your supervisor and be sure you schedule days off regularly. The clinical record is only about facts. It's not a place to vent, not a place to cite your opinion, professional or not, and not the place to engage in guesswork. The reader can reach his or her own conclusion with your use of the **objective** "as evidenced by" (aeb). Report the facts, leave the rest to eternity. We are objective helpers, not clinical police.

One note represents each unique service category, even if multiple services are delivered inside one session. I'll explain. If I engage in 10 minutes of case management and 40 minutes of talk therapy, I cannot bill for 50 minutes of talk therapy. Instead, I write two (2) notes:

1. 40 minutes of talk therapy and
2. 10 minutes of case management

Billing otherwise is considered fraudulent billing, which is legally actionable by the party who pays for the service – insurance company, department of health services, private citizen.

Additionally, the length of the clinical note is important. Too long or too short and you can hang yourself. The length and content of a note is a skill that supervisors assist with.

If you mention something that happened in prior note, synopsize it. Don't send the reader into another part of the chart. This is cumbersome and irritating. Result: If the reader is an auditor or me, that person will find other infractions and ask you to address them as legal and ethical standards allow.

TYPE	DEFINED	
TYPES of Notes	-Therapy -Case Management -Case Consult	*-Directly linked to service plan* -Telephone call or message to/from/about client If cancel or rebook, note the number of time to date that has happened and intake date (EX: 3rd cancel/rebook since 3 April 2020) -In-house consults with sup in any supervision format (1:1, group, triadic)
SOAP Format	Client Subjective report Your Objective observation Action taken Plan for client and you	*Directly linked to service plan* S, O, A: Past tense P: future tense (client will…, writer will …)
DAP Format	Description Assessment Plan for client and you	*Directly linked to service plan* D, A: Past tense P: future tense
LONG Note		*Directly linked to service plan* The longer the note, the more rope to hang yourself
SHORT Note		*Directly linked to service plan* The shorter the note, the less meaning it has and the more rope to hang yourself
JUST RIGHT Note		*Directly linked to service plan* Progress with service plan goals limitation to progress with service plan goals Plan for addressing each

Notation Do & Don't

DO	DON'T
ROI unnecessary within the agency. This is built into the client's general informed consent. In private practices where non-clinical staff may attend group supervision, exercise extreme caution to avoid client names and identifying details.	Keep information between client and practitioner alone Consult in a group format that includes others who are not included in the general informed consent
If client was referred and ROI in place: 1.Thank and alert referral source re client's completion/termination/withdrawal. No details. Document the contact. 2. Alert the clinical supervisor re client's completion/termination/withdrawal. Document 3."P" of last SOAP: Be clear re type of "termination": completion, no contact, withdrawal.	If client was referred: 1.No details even with ROI, unless stipulated on ROI 2. Close client case w/o sup consult 3.clinical note unclear re closure reason or other meaningful detail(s)
Link note to the ISP's specific short-term objective(s) or associated long-term goal	Note disconnected from ISP
Note reflects progress, if any, with ISP objectives	Unclear progress in treatment
Note reflects limitations to progress. Without this, no reason for client to return. See?	Unclear reason for continued treatment
Document ROLE TITLES: client, writer, clinical sup, prescriber. Individuals can be located through the organization as needed.	Camelia Shaheed, clin sup; Vanessa Perry, N.P.
Never insinuate anything in the health record about client, supervisor, other professionals, staff, or others. Client record is about client and treatment,	Speak about others
Document ALL client and client-related interactions, without exception: who initiated contact (from client, from writer), format of contact (phone, message, text, in person), reason, your intervention, outcome, plan. **Do not lump different services in one note to save time. This leads to fraudulent billing.**	Miss important notes such as clinical consults during 1:1 or group supervision. Unclear notes re who did what, type of contact made, when, why, outcome. Lumps different services in one note.

DO	DON'T
When quoting, period sits inside quotation marks – "I can't focus." Combine similar thoughts in one quote instead of many. Include a linking word in brackets to bring it together and use … to avoid unnecessary works (e.g., like). EX: "I can't focus EX: "I can't focus … I was upset [because] I can't predict his reaction."	Place period outside quotation marks or use multiple quotation marks inside quotation marks – EX: "I can't focus". EX: "I can't focus". "Like, I was upset". "I can't predict his reaction".
Document evidence observed with "aeb" so reader draws own conclusion. Note's MSE captured: slurred words, sleepy, trouble speaking full sentences.	Opinion, professional or otherwise. Trying to influence others with the note. *Writer suspects client was under influence.*
Use "writer" to refer to self unless direct client quote	No personal pronouns - I, me, my, our - unless direct client quote
Avoid contractions – it's, we're	No contractions - you're, it's - unless direct client quote
Professional nomenclature and tone unless direct client quote. Edit direct quotes to facilitate reading EX: It was sweet. I couldn't … just say that.	No jargon unless direct client quote EX: Like, it was sweet. I couldn't just, like, say that.
Simple and to the point. Balance communicating what happened without excessive detail	Describe everything that happened so note is overly long
Notes represent the writer and the agency. Ensure grammar, neutral word choice, and professional tone.	Riddled with errors, opinions, and judgmental language.
NO positive or negative opinions about peers or others in notes. If they cause harm, the person has legal rights to compensation. Seek sup about such concerns	Positive or negative remarks are personal opinion and are unethical. If they cause harm, the person has legal rights to compensation. Seek sup about such concerns
Never change a note once it's been signed. Some electronic records will not allow changes after 24 hours. Ethically and legally, I've signed a note I leave it alone and write an "addendum" to correct my mistake. The addendum specifies the date, type of note in which error occurred, what was incorrect and what is correct. EX: *Addendum to 12/22/2056 1:1 note: Clt did not use THC, she was tempted to use THC.*	Changes made without any attention to protocol so that future readers cannot make sense of what happened.

DO	DON'T
Only widely recognized abbreviations used such as clt for client, CM for case manager, M for mother, F for father, etc. When a non-standard abbreviation is used, especially if it can have more than one meaning, the first time mentioned: EX: *Clt: I am sick of bipolar disorder (BPD).* BPD can be interpreted as bipolar disorder or borderline personality disorder. BPD can be throughout the note, **this note**. Another note requires the same method.	Abbreviations without translation
Although hard copy notes are rare, NEVER scratch out what you wrote, even dates. To correct an error: ---One line through the word --Initial directly above it --Date adjacent to the initials	Scratches

In the sample note on the next page, observe how nomenclature communicates MORE with LESS words. Also note that auditors needn't understand therapy. I'll explain. The IRS enters thousands of American businesses daily, from airlines to septic tanks, without knowing much about the products. Audit intent: Did the business bill for a service they could bill for? In this profession, auditors require at least three (3) things to determine if payment is deserved: General principles of practice, specific service definitions, and notes (aka bills). Therefore, note content supports:

1. the service definition
2. the client's participation in that activity
3. the service and time billed for supports the claim that a service was legitimately provided
    a. Reason client was present – linked to the service plan
    b. Note content communicates the time billed for is reasonable. Which would you pay for?

        EX: *Clt described one anxiety coping skill she could use.* Billed 50 minutes.

        EX: *Clt described one anxiety coping skills, what barriers she may face in it's use, and her back-up plan.* Billed: 50 minutes.

    c. Objectively testifies to what client acquired and needs
        i. principle learned - progress
        ii. ongoing need – limitation to progress

SAMPLE

NOTE USING CLINICAL NOMENCLATURE

SUBJECTIVE REPORT

"I've been sad and anxious most of the week.... I failed two math tests."

OBJECTIVE

Client denied DTS/DTO, Change motivation: 8/10, 10 as highest. Treatment phase: action.

O x 4, circumstantial, alert with some psychomotor agitation aeb fidgeting and immobility. Initially lethargic, tearful when she expressed relief father (F) was not upset about grades. Affect shifted from tearful, constricted to content appropriate.

ASSESSMENT

Intervention, Goals: CBT for Goal 1 extracurricular activity and Goal 2 emotional regulation.

IDed withdrawal to quiet space, deep breaths to manage psychosocial stress, discussed positive experience w/ Humane Society, youth group service day, basketball with F.

Clt labelled, modulated, appropriately expressed, processed thoughts that triggered emotions (related to alexithymia). Used feeling wheel to ID emotions. Brainstormed thought states as she experienced them. Sudden flattening of affect at start of exercise. "... [it's] scary" at 8/10 (10 most anxious). "I don't care. I want to know .... I can't walk around not knowing what I'm thinking and feeling .... Bizarre."

"I realize thoughts are a bit scary [which] makes me more responsible, doesn't it? I can sense trouble. My Ma hit me when I spoke my mind. So, I stopped talking .... Maybe stopped thinking and feeling." She wondered if affective incongruence and emotional detachment were part of guilt, loneliness, trust concerns. She explored trust and dichotomous thinking related to writer - she blocked or derailed thought processes to suppress cognitive-emotional expression. "Could be time to pitch that rule. How will I do that?" Despite insight into detachment, clt struggled to ID in-moment thoughts and their impact on self-awareness.

F more understanding than she thought. "Not everyone is my M. That was a nice surprise."

PLAN [for next session]

Client:

--- label thoughts 5 x day by setting alarms

--- compose 1-2 poems on 1-2 strongest thoughts

Writer: 1. consider music in healing

SAMPLE

Consult Note

Consulted with clinical supervisor re telephone call from clt re SI 10 minutes ago. SI w/o plan or intent. Recent change in her schedule triggered helplessness and frustration with others: "Why did they do this?" Clt contracted for safety and stated she had crisis support line number in her mobile.

Sup recommendations:

--- telephonic safety check this afternoon

--- schedule 30-minute appointment tomorrow

--- proceed with support as indicated

--- keep sup alerted re progress

SAMPLE

Case Management Note

TCT clt for safety check in response to morning TCF clt re passive SI, no plan, no intent.

Clt denied DTS/DTO. She used relaxation techniques, especially playing her favorite song. Anxiety level 7 of 10, 10 highest. She will use crisis center or crisis support telephone number as needed until 1:1 scheduled for tomorrow.

THERAPY BASICS

I don’t fear failure because
I don’t cling to success

6

YOU CAN'T SEND THEM OUT LIKE THAT

When considering work outside of session, it is incumbent on each of us to consider certain ethicolegal obligations, not the least of which is informed consent. Feedback and self-disclosures are key and continuous elements of a relationship. Over time, members of the relationship depend on its evocative support and structure,

ETHICOLEGAL OBLIGATION	EXPANDED
	A primary concern about giving, receiving, and soliciting feedback, or making a self-disclosure, is the possible and reciprocal discomfort, pain, and embarrassment. Over the years of doing this incorrectly, we've created a fear of truth. That isn't okay on any level. Peace and equilibrium are too terrible things to waste. While it's true our sense of importance can contribute to the level of narcissistic injury, it's important to work through that unnatural belief. It's also important to realize that others are more generous to us than our self-awareness suggests. People see us, they see us more clearly than we would care to know.

	Self-awareness and emotional IQ aside, incorrectly executed feedback and self-disclosure can decimate or destroy a relationship. Inappropriate constructive feedback is malignant.
Bottom line	Below is not a sacrificial altar. It honors no one, regardless of locus of control ***Do you want to be right, or do you want the relationship?***
	Before the regular feedback or self-disclosure, explicitly communicate ... *Despite the initial discomfort, ...* *I respect you. I believe you can handle what I have to say, if I say it in a way that respects for both us and our relationship* *I want our relationship and each of us to thrive*
1st	Client's ability to understand +/- consequences to engaging in any new behavior – informed consent
2nd	Can you perform this task *perfectly*? Yes is the right answer if you're to verify the client's execution of it
3rd	When providing material in written format, can client comprehend the material?
4th	You have educational context supporting you, what does the client have?
5th	Are the steps clear and in manageable portions?

7

OUTPATIENT TREAMENT: Individual, Couple/Family, Group, Peer, Community Support

Benefits of outpatient treatment include independence, flexibility, and efficient resolution of concerns. The benefits are greater in clinics that participate in *real* integrated care. Such settings – for example, outpatient treatment, PCP, and pharmacy in one location -- offer one-stop shopping, if the care provided by the multiple providers is sufficiently coordinated. If it isn't, the client must return another time or day.

Outpatient mental health treatment includes individual therapy, group therapy, family therapy, medication management, client and family psychoeducation/support, peer support, community support, and intensive outpatient programs (IOP).

Recommendations to clients can get complicated, particularly for timid clinicians. Lives are complicated, especially if clients are mandated to participate in treatment. The better the fit between treatment and the client's capacity to engage in it, the greater the probability of success. In many ways, clients can be "set up" for failure by inflexible systems. By this, I don't suggest bleeding heart treatment. That's not good for anyone. Imagine you're on parole and you must do the following with public transport:

1. find a place to live that your probation officer (PO) approves of,

2. a job your PO approves of, and

3. attend treatment that your PO insists on.

It's something to consider. Is recidivism fully under that person's control? This response isn't straightforward.

Another point concerns which service is provided in which context. I combine group therapy with individual and couple therapy. *Social* skills are learned in social contexts. The greatest change happens in group therapy, not individual therapy. Group therapy keeps the professionals honest. Assuming, we're strong group facilitators, they learn by listening to themselves and their peers, not us. When a client declines group therapy, I can't avoid that discussion. I know the benefits. It's my job to educate but I don't coerce. Time does that independently of me. It becomes apparent in individual and couple therapy, particularly when one partner attends and the other doesn't. Roughly 95% of clients participate in group therapy, especially because I lead those groups. Peer counseling is valuable for the same reasons. I do make sure the peer counselor doesn't engage in a lot of advice giving. Otherwise, it will have the opposite effect.

Group Tracking Hint

VARIABLE	DESCRIBED
Psychotherapeutic	Specific rules Experiential Facilitators ensures equal participation *Thank you, Jack, for your strong participation. I'd like to hear from other group members.* Facilitator makes observations Facilitator keeps group on track Helps group members observe trends and link between sessions
Psychoeducation	Didactic with explicit education topic
Time frame (Linking)	The longer the time frame, the higher the score …
Relevance …	… to group goals
Abstraction	identify themes, trends

VARIABLE	DESCRIBED
Concise	
Klear	
"I"	for thoughts, emotions, perceptions, beliefs, inferences, statements
Needs proof	an observation and an inference
Group focus	not the individual

Finally, don't underestimate the power of community. That's the goal, taking what's learned outside the therapeutic milieu? If clients can't assertively transfer in-session work into out-of-session experiences, then I've failed. Review the ISP, be sure the long-term goals are behaviorally specific and measurable, verify ability to apply skills.

8

SENTINEL EVENTS, CRISES, AFTER-HOURS, OTHER CONCERNS

Agency supervisors have to know what you know regarding sentinel events, crises, and other concerns, particularly at the start of your tenure. ALWAYS alert your clinical supervisor of issues as they arise, even if you don't need help. Most supervisors will let you know under which circumstances you stop alerting them. Some situations will require paperwork the same day before you leave. For most agencies, that's considered essential in the problem re-emerges for another professional the same day, for site licensure and accreditation, for legal reasons, and to prevent other recurrences.

Sentinel Events

Although not all sentinel events are results of error, they are unexpected events that can result in client temporary or permanent injury or death, often impacting not only clients but agency personnel as well. Accredited agencies self-report potential sentinel safety events and maintain a paper trail on each even in a timely manner to ensure continuous client safety. Agencies follow specified protocol and complete documentation that identify, investigate, and analyze events and corrective steps essential to continuous client and personnel safety – the goal is minimize risk and harm.

"Risk" includes any variant of the incident that could include a significant chance of adverse outcomes. "Sentinel" is used because such events necessitate *immediate investigation and response via a root cause analysis.* In agencies, especially publicly funded agencies, that means everything stops for the primary person involved until interviews, data gathering, and reporting are complete. No going home, no appointments. Completing the root cause analysis on the sentinel event is top priority. A root cause analysis ranges from clinical to organizational processes and systems. It, therefore, identifies all the factors underlying a sentinel event with a focus on systems and processes, not individual actions. It also identifies potential improvements in processes or systems that could decrease the likelihood of similar future events or it can determine that no improvement opportunities exist.

Setting also plays a role in whether an incident is considered sentinel. For example, the Office of Mental Health considers the following sentinel events if they occur in a 24/7 care setting: unanticipated death or permanent loss of function unrelated to the natural course of a client's or worker's illness or underlying condition; suicide, homicide, physical or sexual attack; abduction; etc. In an outpatient setting, a sentinel is someone driving a car through a clinic lobby or arriving armed and shooting at will. On the other hand, a crash in a clinic's parking lot is a municipal, not a sentinel, event.

Field Experience v. Post-Graduate Experience

Most graduate field experience supervision differs from supervision for paid employment. Even if the supervisor is unchanged, supervision inherently changes because the stakes have changed – you are responsible, no longer protected by a student umbrella. It is a simple matter to forgive many things students do. Not so with paid practitioners.

DOCUMENTS AND CLIENT INFORMATION

DOCUMENTATION, DOCUMENTS, CLIENT INFORMATION
All client consultations during any type of supervision including group supervision are documented in the client's chart.
NEVER send letters or reports regarding a client without the supervisor's explicit approval of content. Not even to a judge.
Any person who wants client information must have a release of information – ROI - in the client's chart. This includes partners and family members. Client information is defined as any information, even verification that the client is in the clinic on any particular day. If you don't know if an ROI exists or you do know an ROI doesn't exist for the person requesting information, the standard scripted response is: *I can neither confirm nor deny the existence of this person, but if you leave your name and number, I'll pass this note to someone [never say who this is] who can respond to it.* That said, you can always listen and encourage more detail to anything the caller has to say. You simply can't respond to what's said.

CLIENT CRISES

Sending clients to the emergency room or crisis center when they confirm danger to self/danger to others (DTS/DTO) shouldn't be done reflexively. Have you waited in an ER recently? Brutal. Consider the client's state of mind. Now, consider the impact of a 2–4-hour vegetative wait on that state of mind. I've seen how creatively clinicians and clients respond when they're both therapeutically motivated to avoid the ER or crisis center. Sometimes, however, it's exactly what's needed. Never "drop off" clients and return to the clinic. No hand-offs. Other directors may do things differently, but I don't think compounding the discomfort is a therapeutic or ethical answer.

Everyone, especially clients who struggle with DTS/DTO, should have detailed safety plans tailored to their needs and resources. Life spins on a dime. Moreover, clinicians should have after-hour communication methods for such clients. For example, the negative impact of ERs, crisis centers, and inpatient treatment has been well-established for clients with borderline personality disorder. If this group is the cornerstone of your practice, it's important to accept after-hours obligations. Client abandonment can be disguised in many ways.

CRISIS ESSENTIALS	EXPANDED
I've never thought of DTS/DTO	All clients have safety plans, regardless of history. Life spins on a dime.
Frequency of safety check	Start of each session for each client with a safety check. Life is messy and circumstances can change suddenly. A student recently discovered this. Nothing prepares us for a client's suicide. When I sadly became a member of that "group" of practitioners, I saw how quickly client perceptions of safety can change. Some may say my response was exaggerated. I disagree. That protocol has resulted in many opportunities to assist clients who unexpectedly acknowledged DTS/DTO. I'll err on the side of the client. I'm comfortable asking and asking doesn't pose a danger. Not asking can.
Clients who cancel via telephone of text	Safety check
Clients you've not seen for two (2) weeks due to cancellations	Safety check via telephone
In-session DTS/DTO	This is why I have an electronic notebook with each client's service plan. When I need it, I have it at my fingertips. If the client acknowledges DTS/DTO, respond with calm, unambiguous, and assertive direction, alert your supervisor, and tailor the safety plan even more. Being directive is not therapy or warm-fuzzy support. It's directive. Use the crisis intervention method from class, the supervisor, or as dictated by the agency.
Telephonic DTS/DTO	This is why I have an electronic notebook with each client's service plan. When I need it, I have it at my fingertips. Respond with calm, unambiguous, and assertive direction, alert your supervisor, and tailor the safety plan even more. Being directive is not therapy or warm-fuzzy support. It's directive. Use the crisis intervention method from class, the supervisor, or as dictated by the agency. Encourage the client to come in if you have the slightest doubt of safety. Identify a method of contact for the next 24 hours and schedule an appointment between 24 and 48 hours. Meet the client as necessitated by presenting acuity. Client safety comes first, not other appointments or embarrassment about seeking supervisor assistance.

9

BOUNDARIES

Healthy boundaries – I won't call it self-care - and responsibility are topics promulgated in graduate programs that, paradoxically, demand significant commitment from students; which I'm unsure they're equipped to give. In recent years, between a shift in level of entitlement and softening constructs – ambiguous self-care instead of clear boundaries – certain principles have been misappropriated. We'll get into that in a bit.

It is one of many paradoxes inherent to certain professions, in this case ours that if you want to earn an MA in two years, there are 60 credit hours to complete. Self-care can falter in the face of a desire to "finish". Moreover, I've noticed how some approach healthy boundaries too concretely under the soft label of self-care. In fact, I mention this primarily because of potential negative consequences for the clients and clinics, but for student or clinician as well. The table below discusses *some* of the variables related to healthy boundaries in order of importance.

VARIABLE	DESCRIBED
Humility	We are our clients. Our clients are us. If you believe otherwise, life has been overwhelmingly generous. The thread separating us from our clients is that we're not experiencing *that* problem *right now*. Knowing the answer is nice but meaningless. 98% of my clients knew the answers coming in. The problem was *how* to meaningfully resolve their concerns, *how* to push through their inertia. X marks that spot each one of us will experience at some point. Quickly, exchange the lens that sees the client as an "it" with a lens that sees the client as a "thou". Not a good idea to take the client's side against someone in the client's life or agree with a particular action. That isn't our role. We've all made that mistake in our private lives. Joe complains about his partner Sally. Friends agree heatedly. Joe makes up with Sally. Friends are swinging in the wind for what they said. In therapy, we're tasked to help clients unravel dynamics. What purpose is served by aligning myself with Joe against Sally? Help Joe untangle what the dynamics with Sally mean, trends in his life that perpetuate that dynamic, etc.
Social Media	So many have questioned their values and disrupted their lives because they confused social media with fact. The amount of misinformation on social media is astounding. I'm relieved students trust me enough to discuss this topic: Practitioners writing coldly and calculatedly about clients and how to manage concerns such as cancellations and no shows, among other topics. Never take advice about anything from an unknown and non-scholarly source. Instead, seek scholarship, seek a mentor, seek a professor. Social media cannot provide an educated and balanced response. **It's *social* media** - a gossip column minus an editor. Would you ask a mechanic about the costs/benefits of a heart transplant?
Thought, Emotion, Behavior Continuum (T-E-B)	As invigorating as feelings are, we live in a world obsessed with them despite evidence-based scholarship. Even cognitive functions are labelled as feelings. *I feel this contract is weak.* No, you think or believe the contract is weak. Has adopting a clear stand gone out of fashion? Leaning on emotions feels safer? Good. Our obligation, however, is to help clients adapt, grow, increase resilience and emotional IQ. They don't arrive seeking more vulnerability. I'm not proposing we become Mr. Spock, but does therapy need to be reduced to *How do you feel about X?* How I feel – bewildered. Will I teach myself and communicate to my clients how to **think** to change what needs changing? Or will I help them shackle themselves to transient emotions? What is <u>C</u>BT? Thought influences emotion (and behavior) >> emotion influences behavior >> behavior influences thought >> and so on I challenge you - change an emotion without cognition.

VARIABLE	DESCRIBED
Emotional Intelligence (EI)	Generally recognized as a healthy leader's trait. I think it's incorrectly named, but to call it "thought" intelligence is awkward and can be confusing. EI is about harnessing the power of THOUGHT, the power of our brains. That said, traits such as EI are based largely on self-report, which is largely questionable. Still, those who possess it can more accurately apply T-E-B to ID and adapt to intrapersonal versus interpersonal circumstances. First, EI requires empathy, which has significant limitations despite its usefulness. Here's what I know... --Children, teens with high EI have high interpersonal skills, low anti-social behavior. --Adults who have it demonstrate high interpersonal skills and low aggression. --Strong self-awareness: accurate T-E-B assessment and execution. --Strong academic achievement, after IQ. --Strong vocational relationships: negotiation and conflict management. --Strong social capital: socially skilled, empathic. --Strong psychophysiological well-being: healthy choices, life satisfaction, self-concept. Second, to accurately demonstrate EI, two (2) ingredients are key: fearless self-assessment and feedback. Neglect one and EI is dinner conversation. --Fearless self-assessment. Why not? Others see us more clearly than we know. --Address positive/negative emotional states in self and others. Limited or inability to non-defensively and empathically see self → limits ability to non-defensively and empathically see others. --T-E-B warrior S U R V I V A L ----Necessary to *exploit* changing thoughts for adaptation. Hello, lizard brain. ----Emotions are complicated because they're easier to blame than thoughts. Thoughts have the element of volition. Instead of general emotional sensitivity, foster sensitivity to how thoughts position your hands on the steering wheel and your feet on the gas/brake. Exciting and scary. ----Manage, don't eliminate emotions with a muscular brain. A muscular brain knows which thought resulted in which emotion. Humans change to suit themselves. Every decision is based on a precise unconscious desire to serve self via survival. *What can I live with?* Sister Theresa of Calcutta and Charles Manson insisted their visible lives be congruent with their invisible values.
I statement	Good fences make good neighbors. To fully know who's in charge, I use language that reflects that. I speak only for myself.

VARIABLE	DESCRIBED
Continuity	This profession is an continuous process that proactively addresses various life domains that maintain balance, not a temporary piece of plaster applied to a wound. It reflects a mature awareness of basic needs, draws a line as if to say, "*Here and no further.*" In our profession, that consciousness is an ethical imperative. Thus, boundaries come in a variety of shapes and sizes. For example, I *expect* and prepare for bad days. Listen, this isn't knitting. We deal with concerns, often tragedies. Figure it out be it via your supervisor or your own private work. Some bad days last months. Do I abandon my post and call it "self-care"? If clients trigger you to leaving your post, resolve this immediately or find another niche. That's like a surgeon who is afraid of blood. Ethics and licensure require this level of self-awareness.
Ethical Breach	To a directly related second point, a topic of frequent concern among practitioners: If I leave my post because a client "triggered" me, I breach ethics. I knew my triggers before I began work today. Clients trust me each time we make an appointment. I can't abandon clients who seek me for their wellness. What to do? Seek supervision, consider a position where clients can't trigger you. Of course, if I'm ill, I'll leave. But this modern iteration of "self-care" is no more a healthy boundary than caviar is similar to chicken eggs.
Behavioral Interpretation	What, then, does this inclination among some practitioners to focus on self and bolt demonstrate? If instinct matters more than obligation, if the thought of listening and being present for another overwhelms me, perhaps the fit between me and the profession is a weak or non-existent one. This is the profession, not a novel or movie. I don't need to be in the mood. Is my doctor always in the mood? My attorney? My choices impact others. A mentor once said: *Many people want to become therapists because a therapist once helped them through a hard time. They seek graduate programs citing their passion. OK. Here's the problem: Those aren't solid enough reasons to enter a profession. Teachers open the world to us, doctors cure what ails us, financiers increase our wealth, ... But this one emotionally laden experience is what many cannot let go of. I worry. I worry about transference and countertransference after reality sinks in. Passion dissipates, commitment largely doesn't.*
There are more, but I'll end here	Schedule an appointment with your supervisor, advisor, mentor, therapist; remember your boundaries – school or work schedule – are under your control not the reverse. Explore experiences and options. Grab the power of language, particularly the difference between thought and emotion, and strategic use of words. All these are examples of responsible and ethical boundaries. *Self-care*, as it's currently being mis-appropriated, is only going to hurt clients and our profession.

10

KNOWLEDGE TRANSFER

Some points to consider as students transfer knowledge into practice, especially during graduate field experiences.

KEY POINT	DESCRIBED
3 things at the start of the first meeting	**ID client personality**. Immediately, what's the plan to avoid wasted time and bad habits on both sides? **ID client communication style.** What's the plan to avoid wasted time and bad habits on both sides? If the client is talkative, I'll implement redirection technique immediately. *We'll begin with the therapeutic informed consent, the TIC, today.* One of those is will be redirection. I continue: *When we go off topic, I'll make this signal and redirect you. It isn't that I don't want to hear what you say. It's that I'm more concerned about the concern that brought you in.* If the client is quiet, I'll implement the ownership technique immediately. *We'll begin with the therapeutic informed consent, the TIC, today.* One of those is will be owning the session. I continue: *You strike me as a quiet person. I prefer to listen, too. Since this is your concern, the floor is yours, not mine. My job is to keep us on track and help you find the answers to your concern.*

KEY POINT	DESCRIBED
We are clients, clients are us	If you think differently, even in cases of psychosis, then I'm at a loss for words.
I statement	Good fences – boundaries - make good neighbors. To fully know who's in charge, I use language that reflects that. I speak only for myself by using the pronoun "I". "You" diffuses ownership.
Healthy Boundaries	*Consider the following for clients and yourself:* Know your limits. What do you need, when? What's the plan? Consist, direct, and non-apologetic communication about boundaries. Assertion skills required. Know how to say "No". Practice taking care of yourself in a respectful manner. Meet own needs without trespassing on those of others.
Types	Physical, intrapersonal, interpersonal, emotional, sexual, spiritual, intellectual, time (work included), material (resources, technology, personal energy) and non-material (values),
Primo 1: How does that make you feel?	Emotions often get us into and keep us in trouble. Thoughts drive emotions (and behavior) and emotions drive behaviors. Ideally, the human brain is the engine, not the amygdala. We've become mesmerized by something transient. When my surgeon cuts me, do I rely on his emotions or his brain? When my banker invests my money, with what am I more secure – the feeling or the knowledge behind the investment? Let's gird our clients with cognitive fortitude, not increase their vulnerability.
Primo 2: Mainstream social rules and therapeutic social rules	Know the differences. Counseling is a unique environment with unique "manners" balanced against obligations. It's important we don't confuse one set of rules with the other.
Primo 3: Therapeutic Informed Consent (TIC)	The first service that informs the rest. TIC sets the stage for client and clinician about roles, responsibilities, and consequences to certain behaviors.
Primo 4: Counseling is not "processing"	Counseling, regardless of setting, is everything from agency informed consent, intake assessment, TIC, discharge planning that begins with the first session, processing, service planning and progress reviews, future pacing, and concluding. Minimizing the importance of any of these elements minimizes counseling: "I'm sorry, we need to complete this boring part. It's required." Then, we wonder why clients don't engage in sections like service planning.

KEY POINT	DESCRIBED
Primo 5: Transference and Countertransference	**Clients and practitioner can engage in both projections.** Practitioner who regularly demonstrate either or both may be novice practitioners, have unresolved long-standing concerns, are self-unaware, and/or have porous boundaries. Both are often highly subtle concepts in psychotherapy. They are more common in therapeutic relationships than practitioner are aware. Indeed, most practitioner think transference and countertransference are highly evident when they are, in fact, subtle. Hence, they significantly influence the dynamics of therapy. Attachment theory, for example, explains how childhood attachment to caregivers and how those patterns emerge in adulthood. It is often in therapy when clients show their attachment styles – projected on the clinician - as they work through concerns. Thus, understanding and managing both projections are key to the clinician's navigation of the client-clinician relationship, and maintenance of professional and effective service delivery. **Transference** occurs when a client, often unconsciously, projects expectations, needs, and emotions from other primary relationships to the clinician. **Countertransference** occurs when the clinician, often unconsciously, responds/reacts to the client's transference, and from the clinician's other primary relationships.
Primo 5: Transference and Countertransference **Techniques** *Transference*	- ID and understand client/own projections. A variety of modalities can facilitate learning from where automatic thoughts and responses originate. When clients/we ID thoughts, they/we create meaning for emotions instead of struggling to understand and articulate experiences. - Explore origin of thoughts, then emotions. Drilling into the past, even with preparation, is anxiety-provoking work. Even so, the journey has rewards – courage, resilience, empowerment, esteem. Consequently, practitioners are required to be personally and professionally prepared to assist in the "knitting" of this intrapersonal montage. - Client and clinician healthy boundaries are essential for strategic, objective, ethical, and unbiased client care.

KEY POINT	DESCRIBED
Primo 5: Transference and Countertransference Techniques *Countertransference*	-Self-reflection and clinical supervision. Self-reflection and clinical supervision ensure unbiased work. Objectivity is a pillar of therapeutic work with ethical responsibilities. Client and clinician self-reflection introduces objectivity during cognitive and emotional review. A by-product is improved boundaries as well as personal and professional skills. -Clinician therapy. Part of a healthy professional disposition is the ability to discern the need for professional support. Therapy to work through personal traumas, triggers, and/or unproductive attachment styles that may emerge during sessions is vital. -Session mindfulness practice. Practitioner can teach and learn a plethora of mindfulness-based techniques that regulate thoughts, emotions, and behaviors during sessions.
Primo 6: Supervision	Supervision based on supervisee self-report isn't ethical supervision because it's 100% subjective. Observation-based feedback is the only path to professional development for ethical and legal reasons because it is objective. Yes, it's hard to listen to ourselves on recordings and receive constructive feedback, but that's replaced with an urgency to know how we're doing. In fact, it develops into an addiction once practitioner see its positive impact on themselves and their clients.
Aha! 1: Don't deprive yourself of mistakes	Celebrate each mistake. Mistakes fuel self-awareness, learning, and humility. Mistakes remind us not only of our humanity but also that we are our clients and our clients are us.
Aha! 2: Don't co-opt client success	Clients spend one to two, perhaps five, of a 168-hour week with us. Their success is due to their work and heavy lifting. Let's not overestimate our importance. It's been my experience that it's our anchoring presence that means the most to clients. Clients decide to seek help and they do the work. Sometimes, they realize the work will be greater than they anticipated. Change or not ready to change – both take humility and courage. **Nothing** in counseling is about us despite the amount of time we spend studying and practicing. To take credit for client success, which is a source of concern, be sure to take credit for client limitations. One can't exist without the other.
Aha! 3: JOIN before you lead	

KEY POINT	DESCRIBED
Aha! 4: Salary and evaluation	Until you've been paid AND evaluated according to a role's standards, you don't know what you don't know. Please don't disrespect your learning process or minimize the work of others by believing you know what you can't possibly know.
Aha! 5: Self-Concept, Happiness, Symptoms of diagnoses	Self-concept and happiness are by-products of living well. I've seen charts with a minimum of 500 clinical notes documenting the client's and therapist's pursuit of these esoteric constructs. Help clients change, add, or eliminate behaviors. That, if anything, can result in either or both. Keep in mind that some people cannot think well of themselves just as others are happier when unhappy. Symptoms of a diagnosis, outside of DTS/DTO, is the purview of the medication prescriber. Psychotherapy assists with observable behavior, it isn't the evidenced-based practice for psychosis, ADHD, and other diagnoses. Otherwise, we slip into the rabbit hole not to be seen for another 500 clinical notes. Medication can help, although arguments have been made.
Aha! 6: Counseling is the client talking, not the client listening to us	We are the track, clients are the train. We keep the session focused on the 1-2 identified concerns in the service plan.
Aha! 7: Discharge planning	Begins the first session with baseline and stops the last session.
Aha! 8: Don't suffer from nice	Practitioner are required to be many things, but social "nice" is not among them. We have obligations and responsibilities and "nice" interferes with meeting them. People seek our services for what they can't get from others. We have a job to do. This doesn't permit you be unkind. Therapeutic social rules aren't the same as mainstream social rules. Don't shirk your professional obligations. The first 10-13 sessions are the most meaningful. If you waste even one session, your client pays the price. So, do you have personal work to do to reach the bar? If yes, what are you waiting for? Go!
Aha! 9: Clinical assertion, not aggression	Practice consistent centered-ness and assertive therapeutic behavior to assist clients in finding their answers. Everything that happens during a session from hello to goodbye, is strategically therapeutic. No assertive therapeutic technique is ever used too early, including redirection. Are you centered? Are you assertive? Do you know the differences between assertive and aggressive?

KEY POINT	DESCRIBED
Aha! 10: Advice and underwear	Most of us don't share our underwear. It's private, personal, and suits us. The same applies to advice. Be respectful - Help clients find advice within themselves, not your advice. Knowing the answer is non-material because your right answer needn't be the client's right answer. Clients often already know the answer. Yet, they are in your office. True case: A practitioner saw the "answer" to the client's problem and gave advice, the client followed the advice, the client experienced a negative outcome, the client pursued legal action, the client won the case. The urge to advise or give the "correct answer" to a client reflects practitioner countertransference, that some clients take quick advantage of. It requires the clinician's immediate attention.
Aha! 11: Comfort versus safety	Change is uncomfortable because it insists on the modification of entrenched behaviors and the inertia that keeps them firmly in place. If I want to be lean and muscular, I will push through inertia and discomfort to become lean and muscular. Pleasant and inspiring conversations with gym trainers won't make me lean and muscular. Comfort is nonmaterial to such hard work. Safety, however, is essential to such hard work. If I lift weights incorrectly, I can damage muscles, tendons, and joints. My trainer informs me, demonstrates, and oversees my work to ensure my safety. Counseling is not a move or book, it's serious business. Once as I reviewed the record of a new client, I had to read 4 massive volumes covering an equal number of years. She was in more emotional pain when she met me than when she met her first clinician. Each successive clinician had focused on the why of her pain without resolution. No one thought to resolve the pain before the why. I was honest. I told her I was unsure she would ever learn why, if she hadn't done so already. But, I added, I was sure she could resolve the pain. And she did.
Aha! 12: Explain Everything & Verify Client Competence or Understanding	Clients don't read minds. Share and practice definitions, processes, what to expect, … When you ask a client if they understand, they'll typically say yes. Now, verify. Ask the client to demonstrate or repeat what you shared. If you don't, what they do after they leave you is on you.

KEY POINT	DESCRIBED
Aha! 13: Consistent and focused service	Step-by-step protocol: --KNOW assessments before using or interpreting them. It will keep the process efficient and conversational, less tedious. If something is dull – every job has dull parts - rushing through it will cloud potentially important facts. Bored? Don't transfer that to your client, change your approach. -----Before starting, explain the time available, what will happen, and its importance to the counseling process. -----Alert the client you may need to redirect to maximize time together. For example, I alert clients that I'll redirect them when they repeat information or drift into an unrelated topic. I show them my redirection hand signal. --Identify your client's communication style asap. Talkative clients will require redirection. Quiet or shy clients will require a statement about their ownership of the process. This will help you avoid the "attorney-witness" questioning mode as well as a passive client that waits for you to say or ask something. EX: "I sense you don't talk very much. Our work together needs you as the driver and me as your passenger keeping my eye on the map. Otherwise, change will be longer and harder than it needs to be. It may even be boring." --Review the TIC together, if you're going to be the one working with the client, which isn't always the case. Everyone signs and has a copy. Issue later? Pull it out. **--ISP Long-term Goal 1**: Always about safety, even when SI or HI are currently denied (life can spin on a dime). If this emerges in a vocational context, turn to the client's rehabilitation/mental health counselor on the team. At least three (3) standard short-term goals (STGs) for this long-term goal (LTG). See SAMPLE -----I will always *speak* with counselor before acting on SI or HI -----I will not suicide by accident or on purpose -----I will use my support list and strategies each time I have SI **--ISP Long-Term Goal 2**: Start with one STG. There is a 95% chance the ISP will change within the first three weeks. Collaborate with the client to identify a STG that starts but doesn't complete the ISP. --Now, select your treatment modality and begin the talk portion of therapy – keeping in mind the modality fits client needs not your needs - and the paperwork related to it.

KEY POINT	DESCRIBED
Cancellations/Re-books	Each time this happens, write a note. When it happens a third time within 2-3 months, discuss it with the client. See note examples below according to what we discussed during TIC conversation. Please note the non-punitive tone. Clients cancel and things happen in life. I don't punish clients. First cancellation since intake 2/3/2025 Second cancellation since intake 2/3/2025 Third cancellation since intake 2/3/2025. Writer wondered whether a pause in treatment may be in order. Something in clt's life required attention. Clt can address it and return once resolved. Regular cancellations fracture treatment: If something needs attention, give it the attention it needs.

11

ENGAGE, OBSERVE WITH THE SENSES, PARALANGUAGE, HOW TO BE WITH THE CLIENT

Attending and listening are essential components of positive outcomes, regardless of profession. Imagine the outcomes when an architect doesn't attend or listen to the client. To listen is to focus attention on what is heard or signed in sign language. We know a sound is made or something is being said. To attend is to exceed physical presence or the act of listening. One can listen without attending. Attending implies active engagement and participation with the sounds or what is being said.

ATTEND/LISTEN SKILL	
Attend: Foundational to Listening	Skillful attending requires practitioners to listen, not talk. One word or motion can guide and refocus the client. Expert practitioner apply selective attention to maximize the limited time allotted to each session as well as the limited number of efficacious sessions. Like any skill, apply attending sensitively and strategically according to each client's unique traits. That means we don't use cultural principles to let ourselves off the hook when feeling timid about skill application. We find a way. It's our job. Be responsibly fearless.

ATTEND/LISTEN SKILL	
Attend: Listening Skills	-How do we know if someone is attending or listening? -Eye contact (? Visual impairment, culture) -Verbal response: encouragers, clarification, paraphrase, redirection -Vocal qualities: congruent tone and rate to information, culturally sensitive -Nonverbal response: minimize clinician chatter; when attentive and authentic, it's everything
Attend: Listening Specifics, Individual Cultural Differences	A strong start to sensitivity of differences is to describe your unique traits and professional style. For example, I describe self-responsibility and what that looks like during service delivery. That's significant. Self-responsibility implies an internal locus of control that may be absent in the cultural makeup of some clients. How will I negotiate that internal-external difference responsibly? First, note that cultural sensitivity need not, fundamentally, be ethnic or racial. Rather, it underscores individual differences. Family members differ culturally despite global racial or ethnic components. No two people are fully alike, not even identical twins. Second, describe what the service is and is not and describe the similarities and differences in our roles. See how those pieces fit to determine what follows. It's been my experience that I can negotiate differences as long as I'm sensitive to their existence.
Empathy	This is how we enter the world of another and communicate some understanding of their experiences. It allows for some emotional distance since we can never fully know another person. There are always gaps of knowledge and understanding. Take care, since you can ring a sour note when you believe you understand more than you can ever understand. Some things cannot be empathized with.
Sympathy	Emotions generated when one person shares the feelings of another. Here, there is no emotional distance when one experiences the negative or positive emotions of another.

ATTEND/LISTEN SKILL	
Pity	A fully detached experience, neither sharing nor understanding. It amounts to a conscious acknowledgement of the other's plight and, in some measure, an unconscious relief that one is safe from the experience. It can reflect a power differential. Example: In the 1800s, many women volunteered time and money to the poor at local churches out of pity. They had the time and the money that others did not.
Reflection	An honest introspection, not insightful materialism. Can be low, medium, or high levels. **CAN ALIENATE CLIENTS**: if used more than once or twice during the full session, and later than the first half of the session. You can over-use this skill ONLY when the client is ambivalent or pre-contemplative.

Frequent Questions

How long should clients stay in treatment? It depends. Most of the work I do lasts between 10-20 sessions. That depends on the concern, whether I'm providing therapy or psychotherapy, the determined length of sessions, client ability to process. On the other hand, a client who doesn't progress but continues in treatment despite evidence of non-productivity, cannot continue. Continuing sends all the wrong messages. Speak to the assigned supervisor regarding the reasons, who should concern the supervisor. To continue can reflect a variety of concerns: clinical confusion or being stuck, suffering from nice, countertransference, transference, or other reasons. To resolve the problem, simplify the client case via a tight case conceptualization to determine the essentials. Sometimes, treatment will continue; often, treatment will discontinue, if temporarily.

Clients return frequently disappointed with the effect of homework, especially providing feedback or self-disclosing. Before discussing and/or providing clients with FB, or sending them out into the world to practice, fully induct them into the process. There's a chapter in this book on this. Induction involves information and practice. You demonstrate respect when you provide the necessary tools for success. Do this for everything, every behavior you model and hope the client will model. Never release them to practice outside sessions until they've demonstrated competence inside sessions. If not, you can be responsible for negative outcomes.

Psychoeducation as Treatment: Role induction (therapy, case management, venting; client versus clinician roles), ***social skills, diagnoses, medication, correcting misinformation***. Before the first client meeting, read available documentation, especially those on the course of treatment. Don't ask clients to "catch me up because there's so little time." That doesn't flatter you. During the first meeting, does the client know the diagnosis(es) on file? Do you know your diagnosis(es)? A diagnosis matters. As clinicians, it helps us orient treatment based on our designated scope of practice. Prescribers need it to dispense psychotropics, we need it to determine the course of treatment. Is the course of treatment for rages the same as that for anxiety? Unlikely. With respect to clients, to know the labels attributed to their concerns is to anchor the concern within the context of their lives, and not from the internet. To change, humans have a need to know what the problem is. A client of mine couldn't walk for years before she was diagnosed, years full of assessments without clear outcomes. Then, she had a diagnosis. Labels can overwhelm and provide profound relief. What we do is help clients not see them as curses, crutches, or identities. Such responses suggest other client needs.

I freeze, no idea what to say or do. First, unless a client is highly intuitive or has undergone much therapy, the client is unlikely to attribute the real reason to it. Try this: I raise a finger, *My thoughts are racing. I need a few seconds. Please hold...* We both smile, I organize my thoughts, and we press on. Silence is always better than meaningless chatter and questions. Second, shift focus from self to the client to relieve some performance pressure. Third, about 90% of the talking, guided by the professional, should be from the client. Fourth, succinctly reframing or repeating a key word the client used can help. CAUTION: Overuse of reflection, questions, and reframes can *train* clients to be passive, become hyperdetailed, or get bored. It can also derail the limited time shared with the client. Each session is compressed, not real, time. At a minimum, one 50-minute session represents 5,760 minutes or a week.

What is THERAPY? Therapy is a multi-factorial process often misunderstood by clients and many practitioners. It is composed of several phases, *continuously* informed by the past and present, *continuously* informing the present and future, and each with its own documentation.

Boring! To be clear, lack of training gives paperwork its "boring" reputation. "Dull" resides in the hands of the doer. Some practitioners divorce clinical assessments, role induction/therapeutic informed consent, safety/recovery plan, and ISP from therapy. Transfer of that bias to clients impedes client recovery. Indeed, many apologize to clients for the "necessary evil" of those foundational processes. That tactic is unethical, misinformed, and laden with legal implications. It's our job to transform each therapy phase into a conversation that yields rich data if the client and we are to construct the framework against which clients change. *Why?* Each phase informs client and practitioner of otherwise missed essential data. Not even the talk/process phase is without paperwork. Disliking something doesn't remove its legal and ethical necessity. Don't be that person. Work it out.

12

NICE, UNDERWEAR, URGE TO FIX, CONVERSATION v. THERAPY

The method by which we assist may, in reality, demonstrate our own control. To assist clients who arrive with concerns and may or may not see their circumstances clearly, it's important to be clear about what resides within our power and what does not.

The essential ingredients necessary for the professional's growth are humility and the desire to undergo change. Movement out of that darkness into the light can be difficult and fraught with intellectual defenses. Why the difficulty? One, humans don't give up power easily. Two, we are our clients, our clients are us.

Movement Out of Darkness

THE MATTER	REALITY
Bad news	When you first hear bad news, ask questions and note it. Now, hold. Resist the urge to *fully* fix. You can begin a response, but understand you don't have all the information. Indeed, this initial piece *may* be false. It's rare for accurate or complete info to arrive in one package.
Model	Are you good model? In most cases, the answer is no, especially for those who've practiced for over three years without supervision and in private practice. What you don't know about yourself can hurt your clients.
Self-Empower v. Empower	One person cannot directly empower another person. Each of us has personal power that can be galvanized at any moment or ignored for a lifetime. To think I have power to give to another is to believe I hold the power the other person wants or needs. As professionals, we can highlight that fact and assist clients in locating and stirring the power within them. Or not. That said, groups can facilitate power for other groups through action to bring focus on inequality and so on without guarantee of outcome – lending voice.
Housekeeping	All housekeeping concerns are addressed at start of session: Late arrival, cancellations, homework completion, $ if it's relevant
Driver	*I prefer to be responsible for what happens in my life, good or bad. I know my thoughts trigger my emotions, which trigger my behaviors. My skill at managing my thoughts increases gradually so I'm increasingly less vulnerable to others who push my buttons. I know I can't "control" everything in life, but I prefer to know I own my power and I drive my life.*
Passenger	*I prefer to hold others responsible for what happens in my life, good or bad. I prefer to focus on emotions, which can leave me dysregulated across several life spheres. I know it means others will push my buttons, but I like the safety of being a passenger in my life.*
I v. You statements	Own our statements with an "I" instead of the global "You". "You" reduces ownership. This is regardless of locus of control. I can live and work for others because that's what I choose.

THE MATTER	REALITY
How does that make you feel?	Oh, dear. Emotions have their place, but they don't reside at the heart of change. Emotions are not only transient, they're a source of problems. Yet, much power is misattributed to them. More importantly, it results in many engagement problems, including no shows and no returns. Emotions aren't the engine. The brain is the engine. CBT is based on this essential fact. People who live well aren't driven by emotions. They think. Having said that, don't beat up and bore clients with *What was your triggering thought?* Instead: *I'm curious about your self-talk* or *I'm curious about the belief behind that.* Finally, what are you modelling? Do you accurately use thought and feeling words in sentences? Most don't.
Time talking	Stop talking. Listen. Listen with your eyes, ears, nervous system, lizard brain.
Noli pati a pulchritudine	Don't suffer from nice. When you don't suffer from nice, client doesn't suffer because of you. This, by the way, isn't an invitation to be disrespectful or inappropriate. Nice is what friends and some family give clients. It's what brought the client to the professional. Psychotherapy isn't about nice. It's about respect and the sincere belief the client will find her way as long as we apply strategies that assist her in seeing herself more clearly.
Urge to fix I	The urge to give clients the "right" answer or "clinically manipulate" them into seeing that answer is classic and subtle transference. It reflects a clinician's need for control if not the need to resolve personal concerns: *I'm going to save him from himself.* History is riddled with outcomes of that philosophy. First, it's disrespects the client's right to navigate his own change. Second, use yourself as an example. How often do you already know the right answer when you seek advice from family or friends, mentor, or therapist? Knowing the answer, insight, won't buy a cup of coffee. *Doing* is the trick. Third, to be a helper, I accept the client can decide against change. Change is hard because it requires commitment and energy. Give up your favorite habit right now and for the next three months. Scratching my itch through my clients is no way to deliver services. Fourth, if the client takes your advice or bait, it won't last and may lead to legal problems if things go awry for the client. Humans have a need to adapt from themselves. Professionals don't do it all, we can't and shouldn't. Others are autonomous, outside our control. Intrinsically, we are more like our clients than they us. Consider the central nervous system, the lizard brain, and the following: If you find your client resisting your efforts to help, openly or surreptitiously, consider the following: We're guests.

THE MATTER	REALITY
Urge to fix II	---Resentment or resistance is a natural response when any of us thinks we're being coerced or bullied, no matter how subtly. --- A need to fox suggests transference. The right path is a subjective one. Let's not presume someone needs fixing or that what works for 99% of the population will work for the 1%. Court cases are won and lost accordingly. --- If this is a recurring theme in your work, please see a supervisor.
1st mtg: Listen, watch, plan for: Client personality Client communication style	 *In/Dependent, oppositional, aggressive, assertive, passive* How will you avoid treatment concerns related to that style? From the start, kindly redirect, clinical self-disclose or provide FB from the start. *Quiet, talkative/pressured, philosophical, concrete* From the start, kindly redirect, clinical self-disclose or provide FB from the start. Caution re quiet clients and the trap you're likely to fall into
Service plan	Every session, regardless of therapeutic modality, has a focus anchored in a service plan. Many students make a mistake thinking client-centered therapy means anything the client brings in. Sorry, that's a conversation minus tea and biscuits.
What do I sound like?	That's ego asking. Clients don't change listening to us engaging in intelligenspeak. They need us to apply scholarship strategically, fluidly, and invisibly. Yes, they leave if we're silly or do nothing more than repeat (reflect) what they say, think, feel. Many theories and skills are taught in graduate school. That knowledge is our tool for strategic direction - how we enter and help the client navigate the deeply complex and often hidden world s/he who wants to change. Academia helps us create a fundamental structure from which to assist. I've yet to tell a client I'm using DBT or another modality. I'm not keeping secrets. People want assistance. I assist, not talk about assisting. Each word, each skill is a separate thread in a tapestry. Position the different threads to create a collaborative, flowing, empowering, and skilled tableau, not something that sounds "smart" or "professional". Okay, I'll stop.
What does the client sound like?	Clients change when they hear themselves connect experiences and Aha!s.

THE MATTER	REALITY
Advice I	Most of us don't share our underwear. Don't share advice. Unless the client or someone is in danger. If that's the case, advice isn't what's needed. Just because something works for most people, nothing works all the time. Moreover, it's a lovely way to get sued. Do what a true helper does: Get out of the way so clients can find their own underwear.
Advice II	If you must give advice – maximum of once every two sessions – cover each side of the topic with impartiality. Beware of clients who struggle to find answers. This form of clinical helplessness is a seductive trap for many practitioners. Don't give the answers, teach them how to find their answers – underwear.
Client success	Don't appropriate client success. That's ego. I'll prove it. Most clients spend 60 of 10,080 minutes/week with a therapist. Even clients in intensive treatment spend more time away from us than with us. Success isn't about the conduit.

Conversations v. Therapy

CONVERSATION	PSYCHOTHERAPY
Unstructured, un-normed, unverified, fun, comfortable.	Structured individual interviews that determine level of care and appropriateness, verified by historical documents, work, uncomfortable but safe. Adheres to ethics standards and legal statutes. Normed as much as possible
Free-floating – tangential, circumstantial	Inclusion and exclusion criteria
Can be intimate	Prohibited from intimacy
No specific focus, no map	Focused, linked to a service plan
Advise is free	Advice prohibited unless addresses each side
Self-monitoring	Supervision required for many, valued and enjoyed by some, avoided by others. Goal is to internally self-supervise until next supervision session.
Spontaneous	Require preparation
No legal obligations	Legal duty of care, duty to report, duty to warn
Focus on everyone and anyone	Exclusive client focus

CONVERSATION	PSYCHOTHERAPY
I and you statements	I statement
Rare competence in feedback provision and receipt	Competent in feedback provision and receipt, can teach to others
Rare competence in self-disclosures	Competent in self-disclosures, can teach to others
Everyone chats	Client owns the floor, clinician guides, speaks as little as possible
Shared knowledge	Client knows self best
Nice members, confrontational members	Supportive, assertively meets professional obligations without delay
Variable timeline	Generally, here and now
Subjective	Objective
Anything goes	Measured, respectful, strategic
What else?	

13

LISTEN

PERSONAL RESPONSIBILITY - The power of "I" to manage cognitive dissonance, doesn't violate external locus of control.

1. Identify myself as the creator of my thoughts, feelings, and actions
2. Demonstrate respect for others
3. Demonstrate control over my communication
4. Add to the accuracy and quality of my communication through economy of expression
5. Leave room for others to be self-responsible

RESPECT

DO	DO NOT
Own your views & opinions	Advise
Seek out other views	Judge
Listen to other views	Assume/Presume
Recognize views of others as legitimate	Interrupt, minimize
	Let others off hook: Not share FB because you're afraid to share it

Effective Listening

ACTION	DESCRIBED
Be prepared	Necessary for listening; yes, others know when you're not listening
Listening responses	Support & provide specifics re thoughts, feelings, behaviors. Use encouragers to motivate the speaker to continue or not, depending on your goal, Leaning toward/away from the speaker, repeat 1-2 key words, limited paraphrase (no more than 1 or 2 per session) *Yes, I see, Hmm, uh-huh*
Body language	Promote or inhibit the speaker, depending on your goal: Eye contact, Leaning toward/away from the speaker, Open/closed body posture
Interruptions (rude or clinical)	Point of respect. If you interrupt, the other person continues. If other person's speech is pressured, address it immediately with clear examples of why you're redirecting - manage flow of information in available time.
Concentrate	Phone and other distractions are removed in advance
Very brief notes	Key points when there is much data so you'll maintain eye contact
Open questions	To gain greater insight, prompt more conversation. *How did you meet your need?*
Closed questions	Try to avoid unless strategic. Use to strategically manage the flow and pace of a conversation *Did you get what you needed?*
Clarification	Key to later work and avoiding embarrassing questions later

ACTION	DESCRIBED
Paraphrase	"You said… You mentioned… Let me see if I understand you correctly…," Limit this to no more than once or twice per session. It can corrode rapport.
Summary	If you summarize, do it within first half of session and only once. No one doubts you can remember. What the client remembers is more important. Orders & contextualizes story, facilitates executive function & emotional regulation. **Ask clients to summarize at the end of the session. It informs you of what "stuck" or what's important to the client. At top of next session, ask client to provide a summary of the prior session. It informs you of what really "stuck" or what's important to the client.**
Reflection of content or affect	**Statement** that moves individuals to higher level of insight, especially when combined with a behavior. Foundation for emotional regulation, enables examination of emotions. Captures story's cognitive essence, facilitates executive function. *You're frustrated and confused because you don't want to leave the relationship, but you don't have a choice if you're to honor yourself.*
Limit talking	If you're talking, you aren't listening. If you're talking, the client isn't thinking and owning the session For change to occur, clients must hear their own voices
Don't leap to conclusions	Point of respect. Don't make assumptions aloud or privately. Check it out.
Don't argue or lock horns	Want the relationship or want to be right (countertransference)?

14

COMMUNICATION STYLES

Assertive, Passive, Aggressive, Passive-Aggressive

ASSERTIVE	COMMUNICATION STYLE DEFINED
Defined	A communication style that non-judgmentally seeks action in one's own best interests. A persistent pattern of behavior characterized by reasonable comfort in standing up for oneself when the circumstance warrants it, direct expression of wants and feelings when a need is not necessarily warranted, and to do all this respectfully and without denying or trespassing on the rights of the other. While this style is the most respectful and productive one, it has its inappropriate moments - consider it's effect on a mugger. STOP: Not to be used to reinforce one's sense of superiority or righteousness when judging the quality of something or someone (intellectual bullying). *Individuals have reasons for why they do what they do, much of which is unknown to us and the majority of which does not require our agreement.*
Rationale	To achieve personal objectives, to have positive feelings about self and others

Thoughts and emotions that accompany it	Self-respect, confidence, sufficiency, empowerment, relaxation
Thoughts, emotions, and responses from others that accompany it	Respected, acknowledged, some can feel threatened by an assertive person
Evaluating it	Direct eye contact, appropriate body posture, facial expression congruent with verbalization, appropriate not exaggerated or overused gestures, content and needs accurately expressed, timing of response was as immediate as possible and based on consideration of its content, a behavior change request made based on sound judgement (sensitivity and understanding are key factors)

PASSIVE	COMMUNICATION STYLE DEFINED
Defined	A communication style that does not allow direct expression of rights, wants, and feelings. A persistent pattern of behavior characterized by absence of disclosure and frequently results in conceding to the needs of others when appropriate to do otherwise. Frequently based in fear or the belief that the person does not have the right or authority to insist on own rights (opposite to aggressive).
Rationale for it	To avoid conflict, unpleasant or risky situations, responsibility
Thoughts and emotions that accompany it	Resentment, low self-confidence and self-regard, inadequacy, inhibition, guilt, anger, frustration, feelings of superiority, anxiety
Thoughts, emotions, and responses from others that accompany it	Resentment, feeling burdened
Evaluating it	Gently and consistently insist on shared responsibility, reward efforts.

AGGRESSIVE	COMMUNICATION STYLE DEFINED
Defined	A persistent pattern of communication that expresses and demands personal rights, wants, needs, and feelings by infringing on the rights of others. It is often used to reinforce one's sense of superiority or righteousness when judging the quality of something or someone (intellectual bullying), without regard of others' rights, avoids seeking the individual's input in matters where they are free to choose any course. Frequently based in a strong belief that the person has a right or authority to insist on how things are done or thought (opposite to passive).

Rationale	To express sense of superiority or anger/hostility, to achieve personal objectives (at least for the short-term).
Thoughts and emotions that accompany it	Low or inflated self-regard, righteousness, defensiveness, alienation, bitterness, tension, even the score or playing field
Thoughts, emotions, and responses from others that accompany it	Avoidance, disregard, increasing loss of respect, anger, hurt, resentment, confusion, defensiveness, revenge
Evaluating it	Gently and consistently establish and maintain boundaries, reward positive behavior

PASSIVE-AGGRESSIVE	COMMUNICATION STYLE DEFINED
Defined	A persistent style of communication that indirectly and obliquely expresses rights, opinions, wants, and feelings by infringing on the rights of others in an indirect and often surreptitious way. The behavior is couched in such a way that it superficially appears passive, but is later experienced as aggressive, angry, resentful, or hostile. Example: "Forgetting" to complete an important task despite the agreement to do it, followed by superfluous apologies.
Rationale	STOP: This is an inappropriate communication style in all, excluding life-threatening, circumstances.
Thoughts & emotions that accompany it	Temporary control.
Thoughts, emotions, and responses from others that accompany it	It damages relationships, often without the perpetrator's knowledge because others come to mistrust the person and are unwilling to risk themselves or "waste more time discussing it. I always lose."
Evaluating it	Subtle and difficult to see at first. Progressively easier to catch. Gently and consistently establish and maintain boundaries, reward positive behavior

15

OBSERVATION, FEEDBACK, CLINICAL SELF-DISCLOSURE FEEDBACK v. CLINICAL SELF-DISCLOSURE

Most professionals don't know how to give/receive/solicit feedback.

Outside of where I learned how to provide/receive/solicit feedback, I've yet to meet a professional who knows how to execute these skills flawlessly. This should disturb all of us for at least one reason – professionals suggest out-of-session work to clients without verifying and teaching the necessary skills. That, ladies and gentlemen, is where litigation is born.

Never direct a client to use a skill without observing the client demonstrate that skill

Before providing, receiving, or soliciting feedback, do you know how to observe? Observation, especially by the time we're seasoned practitioners, is something we do with our whole body: eyes, ears, nervous system, gut, and tiny hairs at the back of our necks that salute when our professional – not personal - instinct is triggered..

EXERCISE	EXAMPLES/DETAILS
Observe person's face, especially forehead, eyes, lips/mouth, throat, tongue (yes, tongue)	a. I notice you're not looking at me b. I notice you're flushed c. I notice your lips are tight
Observe person's posture and gestures, especially hands and arms	a. I notice you've made a fist b. I notice you crossed your arms c. I notice you keep shifting in your seat
Observe person's voice quality, tone, volume, pace	a. Your voice is soft, I can just hear you b. Your voice is cracking
Observe discrepancies between messages	a. You say you're relaxed but you've made a fist b. You say you like me, but you won't look at me c. You say you want to hear what I say, but your arms and legs are crossed
Observe discrepancies between messages and body language	a. You say you're relaxed but you're restless b. You say you like me, but you won't meet my eyes c. You say you're interested in what I think, but you're nodding fast as if you want me to hurry and finish talking
Check out assumptions and interpretations (avoid labels and judgement)	a. You look angry. b. I'm guessing you're frustrated. c. I see you as reluctant. How do you perceive your behavior?
Share how observed behavior affects you – thoughts first, emotions second, behavior third	a. Your voice is louder. I think *Here we go*. So, I feel anxious and want to leave the room. b. *Phew*. I'm relieved you're speaking to me. I'll keep talking with you. c. Thank you for bending forward, closer to me. I feel warm and ready to have a quiet conversation.

Providing, Receiving, and Soliciting Feedback (FB)

FEEDBACK DOMAIN	ACTION
Non-Judgmental FB...	... benefits the recipient, not the giver, by helping the recipient understand the consequences of a specific behavior or absence of that behavior. It, therefore, concerns the personal growth of the recipient.
Non-Judgmental FB...	... helps the recipient keep specific behaviors "on target" so they can succeed - a key cultural component.

FEEDBACK DOMAIN	ACTION
Non-Judgmental FB...	... increases intimacy since it involves risk. That said, keep in mind that eyes and ears are powerful tools for relationship building and relationship destruction. Therefore, congruence between your words and tone, the words selected, posture, gestures is vital to how the receiver perceives your authenticity.
Non-Judgmental FB...	... demonstrate awareness and humility by checking on the accuracy of your perceptions.
Non-Judgmental FB...	... quality increases as you are more behaviorally specific and timely; or your self-disclosure is more revealing about how you experience a specific behavior.
Non-Judgmental FB...	... is provided as soon after the incident as possible. Time makes erodes details and memory is more unreliable than we believe. When you can't provide FB in a timely manner, wait until the next time the same thing happens.
Non-Judgmental FB...	... is given at an appropriate time and setting. Recipient and provider will be calm and have time to spend in discussion.
Non-Judgmental FB...	... is exclusively for the personal growth of the recipient. If it's intended to benefit the giver, see **self-disclosure**.
Non-Judgmental FB...	... is objective, even in supervision, non-judgmental, not based on hunches or opinion. If that's all you have, you're headed for trouble.
Non-Judgmental FB...	... is a statement, not a question, about changeable behavior.
Non-Judgmental FB...	... is non-apologetic.
Non-Judgmental FB...	... is specific and to the point.
Non-Judgmental FB...	... isn't about "why" the behavior occurred. That's for the recipient to unravel.
FB in group settings	When provided in a group setting, members can be appropriately asked for their perceptions. Be cautious about FB to individuals within group settings.
Steps in FB provision	
1	Ask permission before providing FB.
2	If recipient declines, request a time. If the person avoids FB, make a self-disclosure statement, if you're prepared.
3	If recipient agrees to hear the FB, provide it clearly and succinctly, with a focus on behavior.
4	When done, alert recipient you're done. Ask the recipient to paraphrase the FB to ensure accurate understanding

FEEDBACK DOMAIN	ACTION
5	Ideally, when the FB provider agrees with the recipient's paraphrase, recipient thanks the provider and selects a response from a-e: a. Paraphrase the FB heard, agree with it, thank the FB provider *I don't like it when I do that. Thank you for telling me.* b. Paraphrase the FB heard, request more information or clarification on it as an attempt to understand, not as an attempt to explain why you did what you did. That's defensiveness. Only LISTEN to FB *Could you be more specific?* *What about my being quiet bothers you?* c. Paraphrase the FB heard, respectfully state you disagree it, thank the provider *I hear you say you think I give too many suggestions during role plays. I think I see why you believe that. (don't say "but" – undermines your positive remark). I believe my contributions are valuable. Thank you for telling me about this because I'll be careful not to dominate the group.* d. Paraphrase the FB heard, express your feelings after the FB, thank the FB provider *Thank you for telling me. To be honest, my first instinct is to reject it; but I'll think about it since I trust you.* e. Paraphrase the FB heard, deal with the issue it raises later, thank the FB provider *You're frustrated about last night's meeting. Thank you for telling me. I'd prefer to discuss this further after, rather than before, dinner.*
6	Thank the FB recipient for listening to the FB
Soliciting FB	Integral to self-awareness and humility. Regardless of insight and expertise, there's always room to learn. Solicit FB from someone who can be balanced and forthright. If not, your request is either self-serving or going to provoke an argument. Seeking FB is a genuine opportunity to see ourselves through the eyes of another. FB from others helps keep us "on target" with our goals and it fortifies intimacy. As previously stated, eyes and ears are powerful tools for relationship building and destruction. To be authentic, be congruent in words and tone, posture, and gestures. Demonstrate awareness and humility by checking on the accuracy of your perceptions. Bottom line: to ask for FB is to listen then thank the person who provided it. NOTHING ELSE FOR ANY REASON.
Steps in FB solicitation	
Openness to FB	Never solicit FB if you're unprepared to hear it. If you have difficulty with receiving FB, or have been told you do, you have work to do. FB can't be escaped

FEEDBACK DOMAIN	ACTION
Openness to FB	Solicit FB no more than once per week to demonstrate openness and non-defensiveness. Be sure to act on the FB. Yes, people notice.
Openness to FB	Frame FB as a continuing exercise in self-exploration and mean it.
Openness to FB	Do not look for hidden meaning in FB.
	Layer the FB you receive from others. Where FB from multiple people converges, you have key info about how others experience you. Welcome to the human condition. You don't need to like it to use it. Narcissistic injuries do heal.
1	Don't solicit FB when a. You're not calm b. Time is limited c. Setting is inappropriate
2	Listen actively, not blankly or defensively – you asked
3	Ideally, when the FB provider agrees with the recipient's paraphrase, recipient thanks the provider and selects a response from a-c: a. Paraphrase the FB heard, agree with it, thank the FB provider b. Paraphrase the FB heard, request more information or clarification on it as an attempt to understand, not as an attempt to explain your action. That's defensiveness. Only LISTEN to FB c. Paraphrase the FB heard, thank the provider, don't agree or disagree with the FB. You asked. Deal with the issue it raises later. *Thank you for telling me. I will think about it because I trust you.*
4	Seek clarification and concrete examples only to better understand, not to manipulate the conversation. The FB provider may need time to consider examples.
5	No explanations or excuses. That's defensiveness. Explain only if invited to, but proceed responsibly. Anyone who provides FB should be rewarded for doing so, sometimes even when they were inappropriate in its provision. Not everyone takes this class 😊 It takes strength of character to provide FB.

Clinical Self-Disclosure v Regular Self-Disclosure

Self-disclosure (S-D), vital to relationships, involves risk. Most of us know someone who discloses only when they're upset, which means that person discloses inappropriately. Such relationships end quickly or persist on eggshells. In therapeutic S-D, each person speaks for self, not anyone else, and owns his/her/their experience. A therapeutic S-D has intent – the welfare of the client. It is not about me, but exclusively about a clinical observation. Why would it be about me? Don't do that.

I don't how else to say this, so I'll just say it:

NEVER about me	Unless I committed a faux pas, clinical services are NEVER about me, even when clients engage in transference or get angry with me. Practitioners are trained to manage client transference without resorting to countertransference.
Rasa your *tabula*	*Tabula rasa* exists for a reason. It ensures unbiased and efficient treatment.
Who's got the power?	Each time I share something about myself, I exert my power: I bring the client to a halt, take the floor from the client, shine the light on myself, and force the client to compare her or himself to me.
Why would you do that?	To persist in personal S-D – bringing attention to myself instead of keeping it on the client – flags transference. There's no other way to communicate that the client isn't alone without inserting myself into the picture? If you share, share a client example or what scholarship offers. The only clinical reason for sharing something about ourselves is when expressing concern as part of safety planning. Even then, that's modulated by the focus on the health of the client-clinician relationship. Helping clients feel less isolated with the problem is no reason to breach boundaries or place ourselves center stage. This isn't a private conversation where my story can matter. This is neither private nor necessary.
Scoring or coercion and the bell that tolls for thee	S-D is not the time for to be right or coerce. It's to share information and foster trust. Trust encourages more client S-D. Over time, the greater the amount of S-D, the greater the intimacy; assuming S-D has not been over-used. Risk increases as level of S-D increases -- increasingly private and important data. In therapy, avoid overusing this skill. If you do, you'll encourage client passivity and boredom. Death knoll.
Me-scan	Before speaking, it's important to monitor one's thoughts, emotions, bodily sensations so each can be owned. Is what I'm about to share going to facilitate client growth or does serve my needs – transference or countertransference?
Caution	S-D reveals more of the discloser than may be obvious – as well as the disclose (is that a word?): Whom to disclose, When to disclose, Where to disclose, What to disclose, Why to disclose

S-D NORMS	S-D FEARS	S-D Can Depend ON	FOCUS ON ME, BUT RESPECTFUL OF OTHER
Increased accuracy in communication	Rejection	Attitude monitoring to commit to personal growth	Personally owned ("I")
Know the other better >> intimacy (although unguaranteed)	Losing some aspect of the relationship	Relationship between me and the other. Start small and build up	I accept tight of others to differ from me, disagree with me, not give me what I want. Natural consequences happen, but not manipulatively
Increased personal insight	Others will judge me as unacceptable or unworthy	Nature of information disclosed	Statement, not question
Builds interpersonal network	Negative response, regardless of its size	Level of rapport between me and the other	Has meaning for me and the recipient (directed to the appropriate person)
Frequent S-Ds are inappropriate and burden the listener. Restrict to once per week	Hurting others or that they can't "handle" the hurt (case of rescuing others)	Level of trust between me and other	Timely
Thus, S-D has a built-in system of reward and punishment	Image I may project	Perceived appropriateness of the S-D (time, place, person, reason)	Specific
		My communication style and ego strength	Succinct
		Other's communication style and ego strength	Clear
		My willingness to risk	Non-manipulative (tears, frustration, threats, inappropriate non-verbal behaviors)
		My belief the other can handle my S-D	Connects to a topic via "because"

S-D NORMS	S-D FEARS	S-D Can Depend ON	FOCUS ON ME, BUT RESPECTFUL OF OTHER
		The other's willing-ness to risk	Demonstrates respect, concern, cooperative intentions; reciprocates with other S-Ds
			Share my thoughts, feelings
			Depends on my attitude
			When I'm appropriate, I don't rescue others from their feelings by avoiding S-D

16

NAME THAT THERAPEUTIC MODALITY

Modality:

A **directive** psychosocial intervention that challenges/changes cognitive distortions (e.g. thoughts, beliefs, attitudes), and behaviors to increase emotional regulation. Thoughts lead to emotions, which lead to behaviors, and round we go. Its "problem-focused" and "action-oriented" perspective means clients can ID and practice new information-processing skills and coping mechanisms to resolve concerns. Available in brief format.

COGNITIVE DISTORTION

1. FIRST, educate clients re what emotions are and are not and their sensitivity to thoughts.
2. SECOND, teach techniques that replace cognitive distortions (overgeneralizing, magnifying negative, minimizing positive, catastrophizing) with intentional and realistic thoughts.
3. Help clients respond not react - challenge thoughts that result in unproductive emotions and behaviors.

PHASES (6)

A. Assessment

Step 1: IDENTIFY behavior or need

Step 2: IDENTIFY if behavior is excessive or deficient

Step 3: IDENTIFY behavior baseline: frequency, duration, intensity

Step 4: Excessive: goal is to decrease baseline frequency, duration, intensity

B. *Reconceptualization*: Help client change view of concern, learn to replace automatic negative thought patterns with positive. This stage cements new concepts and understanding – journalling can help.

C. *Skills acquisition*: New thinking becomes action oriented as clients develop healthy behavior patterns to deal with concern. They transition from understanding to applying new concepts.

D. *Skills consolidation & training*: As things emerge, clients apply skills to increase comfort (to convert new behaviors into habits). They evaluate each application with the clinician.

E. *Generalization & maintenance*: Clients are comfortable handling challenges: confident, automatically responses. Follow-up treatment begins.

F. *Post-treatment assessment follow-up*: Continue to titrate client out (2, 4, 6 weeks). Client continues to report on application outcomes. Treatment ends successfully.

Modality:

This is an evidence-based intervention initially intended for borderline personality disorder (BPD) that has proven beneficial in the reduction of psychiatric hospitalizations and treatment attrition. It is beneficial in the treatment of substance abuse, mood disorders, PTSD, SI/para-suicidality, TBI, and bulimia. It is a modification of another modality (______) derived from meditative practice and based on the philosophical dialectical processes of hypothesis, antithesis, then synthesis. That is to say, clients regulate emotions and reality test to achieve balance, distress tolerance, mindful awareness, acceptance, and change strategies.

In short, individuals regulate their emotional and cognitive processes when they understand the triggers to reactive states. This modality aids in the selection of the best coping skills in a sequence of events, thoughts, feelings, and behaviors in order to avoid unproductive reactions.

FOUR MODULES

1. *Mindfulness*
2. *Acceptance and change dialectic* (1st few sessions)
3. *Distress tolerance*
4. *Emotion regulation* (anger, frustration, anxiety, depression)
5. Interpersonal effectiveness: balance others' needs with own, while maintaining self-respect

Tools

1. Diary cards
2. Chain analysis

Modality:

This modality asks a person to recall distressing images followed by direction in one type of bilateral stimulation, such as side-to-side eye rapid movement or hand tapping. It is based on the idea that negative thoughts, feelings, and behaviors result from unprocessed memories. It involves standardized simultaneous procedures: (a) spontaneous associations of traumatic images, thoughts, emotions, and bodily sensations; and (b) bilateral stimulation – often repeated eye movements. Sessions number (60-90 minutes) depends on progress.

This modality is a cautionary EBP for PTSD - debate continues re the precise mechanism by which it relieves PTSD symptoms, with some evidence it may act as exposure therapy. ONLY desensitization component has scientific support.

EIGHT PHASES

1: history taking and treatment planning

2: preparation

3: assessment

4: desensitization

5: installation

6: body scan

7: closure

8: reevaluation

Mechanisms unknown

Modality:

This therapy grew out of concerns that established therapies failed women (gender bias, stereotypes, blaming, unquestioned social norms). Those who use this method believe many concerns are responses to disempowering social forces. It is a set of related therapies arising from a disparity between the origin of theoretical perspectives and those who seek counseling -- females. Foci: societal, cultural, and political causes and solutions to concerns in counseling. Practitioner encourage clients to live in a more social and political way, a trait that keeps this theory in flux. Goals: identify negative conditions, empower the client, for every limitation there is a strength, acceptance, validation, avoiding blame.

Clinician and client are equals. Both, during the therapeutic informed consent, clarifies the role of therapy, the need for the client to own the process and "save" herself, roles, expectations, and responsibilities of each.

COUNSELOR RESPONSIBILITIES

1. Integrates analysis across counseling.
2. Recognizes the client's socioeconomic and political circumstances, esp. mental health care access.
3. Interferes with oppression, empowers, helps men change.
4. Acknowledges own situated experience and circumstances, self-evaluative and responsive. Culturally investigative.
5. Accepts and validates client.

Modality:

This action-oriented therapy emphasizes personal responsibility with a focus on the client's **immediate** experience, the therapist–client relationship, the client's relational network that defines the client's self, and self-regulating adjustments people make because of their full composite. NOTE: This differs from XX psychology despite its influence on the development of this therapy.

Client and clinician focus is process - what is happening, thought, felt NOW – not what was, should have been, or could be. It's mindfulness led by action. That distinction between direct experience versus indirect interpretation increases client awareness of their ability to risk change.

Goal: help clients be more "alive", free of blocks; experiment with new ways of being; free self from unfinished business; and encourage new action instead of discussion – experimental freedom. Action can be paradoxical, experiential, and experimental. A relational approach, reliant on the client-counselor alliance.

PHENOMENOLOGICAL METHOD: THREE RULES

1. *rule of epoché*: set aside initial theories, biases, prejudices to suspend expectations & assumptions.
2. *rule of description*: describe instead of explain leads to specific observations lacking interpretation.
3. *rule of horizontalization*: everything has equal value and significance, without hierarchy.

DIALOGICAL RELATIONSHIP

Practitioner don't heal clients. Rather, clients and practitioner *co*-create self and other *in the moment*. The clinician is aware of own presence and that of the client; surrenders to the moment; is intentionally authentic even during discord; trusts the process; does not rescue client; strategic; and makes clinical evaluations, but without discussion. This is a clear marker for practitioners who use this method to complete therapy themselves.

FIELD-THEORETICAL STRATEGIES

Field theory sees people and events as parts of large systems, not discrete units, influenced by the immediate and the past events including simple factors such as observation. In other words, "other" is necessary to the experience of "self". Selfhood, from which a functional personality results, is achieved within that self-other relationship (explore paradoxical theory). The field has ontological and phenomenological dimensions. Ontological dimensions include environmental contexts in which we live that contribute to our objective reality. Phenomenological dimensions include the mental and physical contexts that contribute to our subjective experiences. Thus, when we focus on phenomenological dimensions, in the context of ontological dimensions, we increase our awareness of our respective flexible character structure. Use of the empty chair role play is one method of increasing awareness.

Modality:

This method helps clients IDENTIFY values and skills associated with them to increase knowledge and live congruently with those values as they face current and future concerns. Practitioner help clients co-author a new self-narrative via the exploration of value history. This style challenges dominant social discourse that can negatively impact individuals.

CONVERSATION MAPS

Re-author identity. Clients are encouraged to examine the history of their values and re-create stories about themselves and their identities to identify important values and the skills to "live" the values. They also identify unique outcomes or exceptions to their concerns that they wouldn't have predicted about the concern.

Externalize conversations. Identity is seen as a social construct, which makes it subject to choice and change. Clients are encouraged to avoid ideas of a "true" self. External conversations separate identity (self) from concern. Strengths and skills are externalized to construct preferred identities. This skill labels the concern so the client can analyze how it operates, its impact on life, and how to approach it.

"Statement of Position Map". Client and clinician collaborate on identifying the concern through curiosity and the key belief that the answer resides inside the client. The idea is to create solutions anchored in clarified values to increase the probability of success.

Re-member practice. Include those who support the new narrative and exclude those who do not.

Absent but implicit. Positive and negative experiences have implicit values attached to them, which contributes to sensation of pain or elation when we fail or stall or succeed. We tend to have a preference.

Outsider witnesses map. Invite the client's friends, other clients, or anyone with knowledge related to the client's concern to "consult". They only listen during the first meeting. Then, the clinician them to share a phrase or image AND memory of similar personal struggles that emerge from witnessing the interview. Finally, the outsider shares how they changed between now and when they entered the session. The clinician will ask the client about any phrases or images that stand out AND what resonated for them. Ideally, the outsider and client benefit from this exercise: alternative solutions.

Modality:

Cognitive distortions, feelings, and behaviors contribute to distress. This active-directive method teaches flexible preferences that mitigate distress. It's about erroneous beliefs, the disruption they cause, and how they can be disputed and changed (clients require clinician preparation for this process). Cognitive-affective-behavioral processes overlap and rarely exist in a pure state. Everything is biased, a fact complicated by how emotions and behaviors influence thoughts, thoughts influence emotions, etc. It can be am endless cycle of distress because of the evaluative layer we add. This method suggests self-defeating cognitive, emotional, and behavioral tendencies can change without review of the past – what can I do now?

ASSUMPTIONS

1. People have innate rational and irrational tendencies.
2. People un/consciously create emotional difficulties and behavioral tendencies via irrational and self-defeating thoughts, feelings, and behaviors.
    a. Clinician asks client to identify irrational and self-defeating beliefs.
    b. Client and clinician assertively challenge beliefs and replace them with rational beliefs. They use cognitive, emotive, and behavioral methods inside and outside the session to foster rational thoughts, feelings, behaviors
3. Objective: despite triggers, we can select how we respond (rational, self-constructive philosophy of self and others).
4. Cognition, emotion, and behavior are not separate processes.

Beliefs & Disputing Beliefs: A-B-C-D-E-F model

A – Separate from belief

B – belief about the trigger

C – consequences of beliefs

D – disputes of A, B, and C

E – effective new philosophy or belief through the occurrence of D

F – new feelings and behaviors appropriate to the trigger either after point C or E

THREE CORE BELIEFS

1. ***Rigid Demands***: We unconsciously overuse absolutistic and rigid "should", "must", and "ought".
2. ***Over-Generalization***: We exaggerate unwanted events while we ignore positive events.
3. ***Secondary Disturbances***: We add to the original disturbance. Over-thinking.

4 IRRATIONAL BELIEFS

1. Demand tendency (success, fair treatment, respect).
2. Awfulizing tendency (magnify events as awful or terrible).
3. Low Frustration Tolerance (LFT): belief one cannot tolerate adversity.
4. Depreciation belief (one event reflects the client as a whole)

INSIGHTS

Insight 1 – See and accept the reality that emotional disturbances at C are only partially caused by the triggering event.

Insight 2 – Regardless of reason and how, holding to the irrational now means holding to distress.

Insight 3 – To improve and stay well requires continuous cognitive, emotional, and behavioral work.

Modality:

This method differs from others in its focus on three Rs -- realism, responsibility, right-and-wrong. Humans share universal conditions, especially when a basic need is suddenly unmet. This method doesn't invest in the past or unconscious processes. It's about need fulfillment for this here-and-now method focused on conscious decision-making and action. The social component isn't neglected in efforts to find a label for the concern. This therapy principally separates the client from the behavior.

Humans, according to this method, have four basic needs, other than survival, to function: belonging, power, freedom, and fun. This method stresses that we control our choices whether they meet the four needs or not. Key to this is the awareness of wants and needs and the choices that meet them. Thus, we're not prisoners of the past. We can decide and change. The therapeutic alliance informs productive connections outside the therapeutic setting. Clients learn to strengthen their skills and relationships with the clinician for use with others.

CORE IDEAS

Action: This method stresses how we continuously learn responsibility through other responsible people. Choice Theory has four aspects: thinking, acting, feeling, physiology. The clinician and client focus on SMART goals to resolve concerns. We can choose thoughts and actions, but feelings and physiology are more difficult (change thoughts to change feelings).

1st step: client learns to use emotions to self-evaluate.

2nd step: client accepts the need for change, accepts change is possible via a SMART plan.

3rd step: clinician helps the client create a personal SMART plan.

Behavior: A marker for life satisfaction and function. Clients can choose to change their thoughts.

Control: As key to this method as it is to survival. Choice theory holds we can only control ourselves. Controlling others results in frustration and alienation from others. Outside of the fact that we can't control everything, if we believe others control us, we may become paralyzed, frustrated, and angry. In most cases, we choose. This method honors the client's control needs and the same for others.

Present & Future Focus: Practitioner don't dwell on the past because current behaviors are rooted there. Clients analyze their "Quality World" and how it intersects with the same of others. Is it realistic? Relationships make that harder to answer.

PROCESS

Involvement: Rapport is key since the clinician may be the only person who can patiently cope with the client, or the client needs a more positive influence.

Evaluate Current Behavior: The *client* judges own current behavior, sometimes with some encouragement from the clinician.

SMART Plan Possible Behavior: The client develops this to own it. Start small to increase confidence. The alliance bridges the client to new behaviors.

Commitment to the SMART Plan: The client will commit. Include this as part of the therapeutic informed consent.

"No Excuses, No Punishment, No Giving Up": If not this one, where's the other?

Modality:

This non-directive therapy uses a tray, sand, and objects and miniature figures to plumb the unconscious, children or adults. This therapy can be used individually, between couples, and during family sessions. In fact, the process is reminiscent of structural family therapy. It allows the client to freely create scenes with the sand and objects to encourage healing through the process itself. The physical limits of the tray can symbolize personal and interpersonal limits when boundary concerns are suspected. When a family works on a sand tray, the clinician can observe alliances and who selects which object to integrate into the scene. The clinician typically watches without providing much input. The intent is to provide a safe and free zone for the client and imagination, symbolic play that sometimes includes client verbalizations. When the client completes the scene, the client may or may not discuss it. In response, the clinician, without touching the tray, can make supportive comments that exclude interpretation. The clinician leaves the scene to exert its own influence.

Modality:

This is a goal-directed collaborative approach that relies on precise questions that "build" solutions from past successes as efficiently as possible. This method is considered brief therapy with 2-6 economical sessions. This therapy is judgement-free, increases self-determination, and uses the client's language. present and future built upon exceptions and past successes. The focus is the exclusive concern, without concern regarding the history or "why". References to the past tend to be met with empathy only, not processing.

ASSUMPTIONS

1. Clients are experts in their lives, know how to achieve goals. Practitioner are experts on questions that evoke change, without teaching or advising (curious not "knowing").
2. "If it isn't broken, don't fix it". If a client believes something is fine, we don't encourage therapy.
3. Clients are motivated to change. We uncover what it is the client is motivated to change.
4. No need to understand the problem to create a solution. The causes may be complex, but solutions needn't be.
5. Small changes can catalyze big changes.

Process: Help clients resolve concerns without assessing the problem. Doing so only distracts the client from the solution. So, this modality builds solutions or alternatives. It doesn't identify and eliminate the problem.

1. *Miracle and tracking questions*: Invites the client to describe how the future will be different without the concern. Clients measure and track their own experience, in a non-threatening way, to identify differences as they progress. Clients very specifically measure and scale to see their movement from baseline.
2. *Exception seeking questions*: The intensity of concerns fluctuates naturally. Practitioner encourage clients to identify when concerns ebb to maximize their frequency.
3. *Coping questions*: Assist clients in identifying missed resources. Be genuinely curious without controlling or contradicting client perceptions.
4. *Problem-Free talk*: Explore problem-free life domains to reveal resources, to help the client relax or increase motivation. Any life experience is fair game to uncover values, beliefs, and strengths.

Skills NOT Modality:

This set of skills relies on fundamental skills taught in a basic graduate skills course. This technique strategically applies those select skills when a client demonstrates ambivalence about something. No ambivalence, no need for this technique. No discussion.

The fundamental skills are the following:

1. Listen and affirm

2. Mostly open-ended questions

3. Clarification

4. Paraphrase and summarize: summarize only once and before the first half hour. Client summarizes the session at the end and opens the next session with a summary of the prior.

5. Reframe

6. Highlight discrepancies

7. LOTS of reflection, **which kills regular sessions**

8. Resolve any discord I may have created (previously resistance)

Ambivalence is a state of conflicted reactions -- the person has indecisive and uncertain mixed thoughts, is pulled toward **and** away from something or someone. Both sides have equal pull and push ranging from pleasant to highly unpleasant.

EX: I want to lose weight, but I dislike exercise.

EX: If I don't change my diet, I'll die from a heart attack.

EX: I want to weight train, but I don't want to get bulky.

EX: If I don't testify, I'll go to prison without parole.

EX: If I testify, something awful will happen to me, my family, or both.

17

TREATMENT PILLARS: MENTAL STATUS EXAM, STAGE OF CHANGE, MOTIVATION, RISK

The mental status exam (MSE) has a history that I won't explore. Suffice it to say that for therapists, it's the equivalent of the PCP's weight, blood pressure, temperature data collection. The MSE is used by psychiatrists, psychologists, family and emergency physicians, counselors, social workers, and other professionals that need to assess mental status.

Typically, graduate students are introduced to the general concept of MSE and, depending on the graduate program, may delve further into the nomenclature. The setting as well as the duration of the client-clinician relationship will, obviously, influence the level of MSE use. For example, a psychiatric inpatient setting will rely on the MSE more heavily than an IOP.

Many question the need for diagnoses and the nomenclature found in the MSE. They view medical labels as barriers that impose some level of judgement and interfere with client-counselor communication. It's a fair point. Still, it's also fair to note the value of professional nomenclature and the buffers it provides clients. It's important to note that judgmental labels are frequently unearthed by dedicated professionals and ethicists who challenge their continued use. You may have observed how many professions have had their consciousness raised as "unfriendly" language is removed. It's not a perfect system but life is perfectly messy.

It's individuals who wield language in ways that add and detract value and judgement. How we use language can determine its efficacy. I hope my meaning is clear. At any rate, most clinics today use electronic health record (EHR) software that offers MSE options. Many students, therefore, are never introduced to or fully integrate terms frequently found in psychiatric and psychological assessments. It's a shame. Professional nomenclature ensures confidentiality. Language, all language, is important. In my session, even a grunt can prove invaluable.

That said, the following are some benefits derived from clinical nomenclature:

1. Provides the necessary focus for best-fit intervention. If I say tangential, I needn't say *diverges from a topic or focus and does not return, erratic*

2. Provides confidentiality protective factors. There's nothing "juicy" about reading a technical note.

3. Clinicians are ethically bound to review all paperwork with clients before providing copies. In this way, clients are not distressed by what they think they understand. The rationale - Some familiar words have alternate meanings when used in a therapeutic context.

Thus, the MSE is a method by which one clinician communicates the client's state during a session or meeting, a specific point in time. Each document is neutral, supported with observable behavior, and treated with the respect required of any legal document. Opinion has no place in documentation. Indeed, it can create a great deal of trouble if the case enters court. Stick to facts.

The MSE is typically completed by each person who interacts with the client. If three people interacted with a client, three notes are completed by each person, or one note signed by all three people, assuming they agree on the content. In due course, a review of the client's record would provide a picture of the client **across time** as well as the client's response to different interventions and settings.

An MSE can be broken down into categories of appearance, behavior, motor activity, speech, mood, affect, thought process, thought content, perceptual disturbances, cognition, insight, judgment, and capped with lethality. Each category assesses a different sphere of mental function, always noting if the current presentation deviates from the client's baseline. The clinician's impressions, although not completely free of bias, are considered objective. The same clinician can capture the client's subjective impressions in an adjacent part of the clinical record,

Function. Each category of the MSE can be further broken down based on each client's clinical picture. Each section below describes the category and notation nomenclature in gray. Flag evidence of possible neurocognitive disorders and consider an appropriate referral.

CATEGORY	DESCRIBED
Appearance	This category captures the client's appearance during the interaction being documented. Appearance is concerned with appearance of age (appears older or younger than stated age), tattoos and scars, attire, grooming/hygiene. A younger than stated age appearance may be due to a developmental delay. An older than stated age appearance may be due to a medical condition, unmanaged mental condition, substance use, or home status. Tattoos and scars can reflect personality, style, history, or behavior. It's key to establish rapport before seeking details about scars. Scars can reflect accidents, self-harm (e.g., needle tracks, superficial cutting, suicide attempts) or harm from others. Attire can be age-appropriate or not or can be provocative. Although grooming and hygiene reflect level of function, compare presentation with the client's baseline level, if possible. For example, if a client's appearance is unkempt and odorous when it is typically within standard limits, something may have happened or a change has occurred (e.g., exacerbation of a current condition, a new condition). casual, appropriate, chrono & apparent age, ethnicity, height, weight, manner of dress, grooming, hygiene, unkempt, body modification, tattoos, malnutritioned, stains, dental erosion, a rash around the mouth, track marks, gait, motor coordination
Eye contact	Good, avoidant, hesitant
Orientation	Alert, responsive; oriented to: 1 person, 2 place, 3 time, 4 situation ("O x 4" for all)
Alertness	sleepy, alert, tired, dull & uninterested, highly distractible
Attitude	interactive, un/cooperative, hostile, guarded, suspicious, regressed, oppositional/defiant, submissive, defensive, open, friendly, candid, subdued, shy, evasive, negative
Rapport	easy, initially difficult but easier over time, difficult to establish, tenuous, easily upset

CATEGORY	DESCRIBED
Behavior	This category captures observable behaviors during a specific meeting. When a behavior is indicated, it's important to note "as evidenced by" (aeb). If you say a client is anxious, describe what led to that conclusion if not per client self-report. For example: "restless aeb by wringing of hands, leg movement". There can be other reasons. Here in the American southwest, heat can agitate as well as deflate individuals. Observe acutely. Interaction with the clinician is noted here: cooperative, uncooperative, non-responsive to redirection. One point often forgotten in our business is that clients can have reasons for negative engagement. How would you respond to court-mandated treatment? Lack of cooperation is a natural response to restricted freedom, something not to be pathologized. If the client arrives with parents previously described as controlling, I'd expect a change in client behavior. Contextualize what you observe with what you previously saw. If the client's subjective report differs from the clinician's, the clinician maintains neutrality of reporting. For this category, observe client presentation and behavior, flow of thought, and mood sluggish, impulsive, EPS, tremor, dystonia, akathesia, verbal/physical tics, echopraxia, cataplexy, steriotypies, psychomotor agitation/retardation hyper/hypoactive, stupor, aloof, indifferent, depressive, aggressive, exhibitionistic, seductive, lethargic, needs minor/considerable reinforcement/soothing
Subjective Mood (per client)	This category captures the client's subjective perception. Quote the client and note observations that contradict the client's report. Depressed, anxious, neutral, dysphonic, euphoric, angry, apathetic, alexithymic, anhedonic, irritable, sullen, relaxed, fearful
Objective Affect (per clinician)	This category captures the clinician's perception of the client's non-verbal expression – euphoric, euthymic, flat, anxious, irritable, agitated, constricted, blunted, in/congruent with reported mood, appropriateness to the situation, and labile among many others – and its range (minimal, moderate, high). Affect can be influenced by context (e.g., substances, trauma, shock). Therefore, exercise caution when formulating a diagnosis. congruent w/ subjective mood, neutral, dysphonic, restricted, euphoric, angry, anxious, apathetic, alexithymic, anhedonic, in/appropriate, in/congruent w/ thought content, intensity [normal, blunted, exaggerated, heightened, dramatic], reactive, im/mobile, flat, constricted, fixed, labile, wide range, constricted, un/reactive

CATEGORY	DESCRIBED
Motor Activity	This category captures client movements, their speed, and other traits (e.g., gestures, gait, dominant body posture, amount of motor activity, unusual mannerisms) during a specific meeting. Motor activity can suggest a mental illness, neurological disorder, vitamin deficiency (iron in restless leg syndrome), or response to medication (e.g., akathisia, tardive dyskinesia). Motor activity can range from psychomotor retardation/bradykinesia to normal to psychomotor agitation/hyperkinesia. Psychomotor agitation can suggest a manic episode or a response to stimulants. Observing the patient's gait is crucial. A stiff, shuffling, or ataxic gait can suggest a neurological concern (e.g., Parkinson's disease). Prolonged posturing can suggest catatonia or inflexibility typically linked with psychosis. An inability to be still, hyperactivity or impulsivity are often present in attention-deficit hyperactivity disorder. Extrapyramidal response (EPR) to antipsychotics include rigidity, tremors, teeth grinding, tongue protrusion, lip smacking, or the rare and dangerous rigidity of the laryngeal muscles. Hands: Unusual gestures? Tight or relaxed? How are the skin and nails? Any unusual picking, scratching, or rubbing? Tremors can be secondary to anxiety, neurological conditions as well as side effects to medications. Look for unusual mannerisms unrelated to standard goal-directed activities as opposed to the now rare stereotypies, which are not goal-directed (e.g., posturing or posing, turning away, make the peace sign, clicking heels together as one student did in one of my classes). dominant body posture, amount of motor activity, akathisia, tardive dyskinesia, psychomotor retardation/bradykinesia, psychomotor agitation/hyperkinesia, stiff gait, shuffling gait, ataxic gait, catatonia, inflexible, hyperactive, impulsive, rigidity, tremors, teeth grinding, tongue protrusion, lip smacking, unusual hand gestures, picking, scratching, rubbing, tremors, mannerisms unrelated to standard goal-directed activities, stereotypies (posturing or posing, turning away).

CATEGORY	DESCRIBED
Speech product, not content	This category passively captures the client's speech across the meeting and is congruent with the individual's personality. Of special interest are amount, volume, speed (e.g., pressured), tone (ebullient, dull), fluency (language barrier or word-finding difficulty), and rhythm (clear, slurred). Clients with hearing impairments may often ask you to repeat yourself or speak at a higher volume. normal rate/volume, spontaneous, loud, soft, fast, slow, pressured, delayed, retarded, slurred, aphasic, echolalic, stuttering, cluttering, mute, neologistic, latency [slow, quiet, hesitant], normal rate and volume, pressured, slow, accent, enunciation quality, loud, quiet, impoverished, ebullient, dull/flat, child-like from an adult
Thought Process	This category captures how a client organizes thinking before expression. Normal thought processes are linear and goal directed. Irregular thought processes are tangential, circumstantial, loose, perseverative, flight of ideas, and thought blocking. These processes can obviously impact speech. quantity, tempo, coherence: within standard limits (WSL), perseverative, tangential, flight of ideas [FOI], retarded/inhibited, poverty of thought, perseverative, interrupted, disorganized, blocking, fusion, loose associations, derailment, circumstantial, confabulation, ideas of references, magical thinking, depersonalization, grandiosity, illogical

CATEGORY	DESCRIBED
Thought Content	This category captures the substance of thoughts across the specific session. Content can be preoccupied, perseverative, delusional (persistent false beliefs *not part of the cultural belief system*), parasuicidal, suicidal, and homicidal. See the lethality category further below. Practitioners verify client safety at the start of each session and document to it: "Client denied suicidal thoughts.", "Client acknowledged passive suicidal ideation and denied intent." Note the specificity. Always alert your clinical supervisor when a client confirms suicidality or homicidally. The supervisor is likely to recommend a comprehensive risk assessment. Until the client agrees to a safety plan or transitions into another level of care, the clinician remains with the client. Otherwise, the client may leave and act on the expressed intent. Remember: Practitioners, including students, are mandated reporters and California Supreme Court case Tarasoff v. Regents of the University of California ruled that mental health professionals must warn individuals if a client threatens suicide or homicide. In case of homicide, the police are alerted so they can alert the intended victim(s). Delusions can be grandiose, paranoid, persecutory, bizarre, and somatic. It's unwise to ask a client if the client is delusional. That lacks subtlety and sounds judgmental. Rather, ask if the client is worried about X. When determining if a belief is a delusion, compare the client's belief to pre-exiting data. There may be an element of truth to the delusion. Once again, context is important. Moreover, cultural competence is imperative - believing in God can be reality or a delusion depending on the individual. WSL, preoccupied, delusions [persecutory, paranoid, reference, grandiose, erotomanic, mood in/congruent, guilt, poverty, nihilistic], preoccupied, overvalued ideas, obsessions, ruminative, thought insertion/withdrawal, thought broadcasting, somatic passivity, suspicious
Perceptions	This category captures what clients perceive. Some clients may deny hallucinations, for example, out of fear or other reasons. Sometimes, a client denies hallucinations, but is clearly responding to something in the environment, unperceived by the clinician. A hallucination can be an auditory, visual, tactile, olfactory, and gustatory experience of something nonexistent. Auditory and visual are most common while the others can signal a brain anomaly. Hallucinations can be hypnagogic - occur when falling asleep - or hypnopompic - when awakening. Again, context and cultural competence are key. A client who believes God warned him about swimming today can still be reasonable depending on history. An illusion is a misperception of a real stimulus - seeing a face in the wood grain of a door. Finally, drugs can mimic psychosis. WSL, illusions, delusions, paranoia, hallucinations, illusions, pseudo hallucinations, depersonalization, de-realization

CATEGORY	DESCRIBED
Cognition	This category captures orientation, alertness, concentration, memory, abstract reasoning. Orientation refers to awareness of situation, time, place, person (O x 4). Substance use or delirium can interfere with orientation. Delirium is often misdiagnosed or missed altogether. Alertness refers to level of consciousness: alert, somnolent, stuporous, comatose. Altered consciousness may suggest a head injury, substance use, or delirium secondary to a medical condition. Concentration refers to ability to focus. Some tests ask clients to spell a word forward and backward. Anxiety, depression, poor sleep, or neurocognitive disorders can impair concentration. Prescribers, more than clinicians, test concentration in this way. Memory includes immediate or delayed recall, recent memory, long-term memory. Again, this is more likely performed by a prescriber during evaluation. Impaired recall can signal a neurocognitive disorder. Abstract reasoning refers to the ability to consider and infer meaning from complex concepts. Also more likely performed by a prescriber during an evaluation. Literal client interpretation indicates concrete thinking seen in many psychiatric disorders, intellectual disabilities, and neurocognitive disorders. alert, clouded, drowsy, stuporous, attentive, un/focused, memory, executive function, in/attentive, distractible, delirium, dementia, intoxication.
Intellectual Ability	Below average, average, above average, impaired
Insight	This category captures a client's understanding of own condition, described as poor, limited, fair, worsening, or improving. If a client does not realize that his partner is dead instead of being "kept" from him, the client has poor insight. High, Medium, Low, Absent
Judgement	This category refers to the ability to make sound decisions. This is often assessed via the initial assessment. Judgement is poor, limited, fair, worsening, or improving. If a client repeats the same mistakes, the client has poor judgement. Medication adherence can be a tricky point. Some clients believe medication harms them or "I don't feel like myself". Yet others adhere to medication to avoid relapse and inpatient treatment or court mandated treatment. Poor judgment and low function are often consequences of severe mental illness or cognitive disorders. Once again, context and cultural competence are key. sound, reasoned, responsible, impulsive, executive function, impaired.

CATEGORY	DESCRIBED
Risk & Acuity: **Suicidal Ideation (SI), Danger to Self (DTS)** **Homicidal Ideation, Danger to Others (DTO)**	This category captures the likelihood of a client's intent to suicide or homicide. Always check lethality even among clients who consistently deny it - circumstances can change quickly and dramatically. *Especially check it, via telephone if necessary, when clients have been absent for longer than one week.* SI and HI can be passive or active. Active SI/HI can include a plan, means, and a time frame. denied, passive, parasuicidal gesturing, ideation only, ideation w/ plan, ideation w/ plan and intent, unclear plan w/o intent. "Client denies DTS/DTO" DOCUMENT EACH SESSION
***Treatment Phase**	Pre-contemplation, contemplation, action, maintenance. DOCUMENT EACH SESSION
***Motivation**	Client chooses from 1-10, 10 being highest. This naturally fluctuates. If "5" or lower, address the ambivalence. If you don't, all the work you do together will be for nothing. DOCUMENT EACH SESSION

18

TREATMENT PREQUEL: PLAN FOR CLIENT PERSONALITY, COMMUNICATION STYLE

Before we begin, a few words on treatment without rose-colored glasses. Typically, students enter graduate programs with wide-eyed perceptions about clinical work. Up to that point in their lives, they'd dispensed advice to friends and family; perhaps been encouraged into the profession for their abilities to listen and advise. Then, in Counseling Skills and Techniques they learn clinical work requires lots of listening, use of silence, and no advising unless the client acknowledges DTS/DTO. This is tough on them, and on faculty. The apple cart wobbles. Will it topple? It depends. In most cases, no.

Treatment Wobble

The realization that clients aren't receptacles for clinician wisdom can be a narcissistic injury. Therapy is a process comprised of at least eight phases? Say it isn't so. It's so and not one is more important than another. Unless the clinician makes it so. Not one is more exciting than the other. Unless the clinician makes it so. Not one is more boring or "a necessary evil" than the other. Unless the clinician makes it so. Sadly, many clinicians make it so and encourage clients to join them. Direct consequence: Bored clinician **and** client. Out the window -- All we know about the sequential and intersectional contribution of each phase to the process known as recovery. Please don't do that.

THERAPY PHASE	DESCRIBED
Therapy Prequel	Plan for Client Personality, Client Communication Style
Treatment Phase I	Assessment & Diagnoses
Treatment Phase II	Role Induction/Therapeutic Informed Consent
Treatment Phase III	SMART Individual Service Plan
Treatment Phase IV	Talk/Process/Ambivalence/Change
Treatment Phase V	Functional Assessment & Case Conceptualization
Treatment Phase VI	More Case Conceptualization & Service Planning
Treatment Phase VII	Future Pacing
Treatment Phase VIII	Transfer, Completion, Closure, Withdrawal & Closure

19

TREATMENT PHASE I: ASSESSMENT & DIAGNOSES

Includes the initial; and annual updates, updates for each inpatient hospitalization

See italics for the information that's needed. When reviewing an intake or assessment form with a client, the headings and questions are intended to guides the interviewer regarding the spirit of the question. If the interviewer concretely asks questions without going deeper, much is missed in the moment and time will be needed later to gather it. Be curious, but not so much as to become mired in detail. This phase is the backbone of treatment, not a "necessary evil" as one supervisee once referred to it - for the one and only time.

SAMPLE

INTAKE ASSESSMENT

Primary concern: *What was the triggering event? Why not last month or next month?*

TREATMENT HISTORY

How many times, reasons, how long, resolved or not, diagnoses, what stuck with you, psychiatric medication, family mental health or behavioral concerns

SAFETY

Has anyone in your family or close circle of friends hurt or killed themselves or someone else?

Have you ever tried to hurt or kill yourself or someone else? If yes, how many times? When was the last time? How did you do it?

Has anyone ever tried to hurt or kill you? When? How? You're still here, but what was the outcome?

SUBSTANCE USE (includes low alcohol drinks and vaping):

Last use, frequency in one week, amount each use

MEDICAL

Medical conditions that include infections, hereditary or other medical conditions that tend to appear in the family

Physical pain, treatment, how long:

No pain 0 1 2 3 4 5 6 7 8 9 10 **Much pain**

Sleep, appetite, weight

DIET/NUTRITION

What is one word that describes your diet?

What did you have yesterday for breakfast? Lunch? Supper? Snacks?

SLEEP

How many hours of sleep do you get?

How do you sleep?

What is one word that describes your sleep?

MARITAL/SOCIAL

Marital/Romantic status, length, satisfaction

Number of in-person friendships, how many older than two years, ease of starting and keeping friends?

Looking back, has anyone taken advantage of you or treated you unkindly?

LEGAL

Number of arrests, dates, reasons.

Have you ever set anything on fire? Have you ever hurt animals? (What is the intent of these two questions?)

STRESS

Frequency of stressful events, most recent stressful event, describe how you resolved it, what was lesson learned?

EDUCATION/EMPLOYMENT

Highest completed degree, in what?

Current job; number of promotions, demotions, terminations

If unemployed, date of last job, doing what?

Interest in work **None** 0 1 2 3 4 5 6 7 8 9 10 **Much**

DIFFERENTIAL DIAGNOSES

DISCUSSION POINTS
A good proportion of MA level diagnoses fall short when compared with prescriber evaluations. That fact suggests, at a minimum, a training concern -- Prescribers are thoroughly trained in diagnostic and psychopharmaceutical interviewing, graduate level clinicians rarely are. The decisions prescribers make have a more serious and long-term impact on client welfare.
Many clients enter treatment with a diagnosis bias – they believe they know what their diagnosis is. There are many reason that clients do this, not all are manipulative or for personal gain. Psychotherapy has a simple goal – an objective and accurate assessment, regardless of client reports or, even, documentation. There is such inter-rater inconsistency in diagnostics. This is why it's important to read the record, especially the psychiatric evaluation. Not to be swayed but to ensure a full profile of the client.
The self-diagnosis bias has clinical implications if the professional assessing the client accepts that information on face value. NEVER DO THIS. Professionals verify diagnoses.
Human nature: We always believe we're right, especially when it comes to ourselves. That's inaccurate, especially when it comes to ourselves.
Assess clients based on whether they're currently taking prescribed or herbal medication for a psychiatric condition or if not.
Clients unmedicated for a specific condition: If a client tells you he believes he has ADHD, is he more or less likely to answer "yes" to your regurgitation of ADHD symptoms? More likely. So, DON'T DO THIS. Why? Clients will instinctively, sometimes intentionally, cognitively restructure fit your questions to their bias. What to do, then? Observe concentration, focus, restlessness level, etc. Instead of questions, say: Please complete this survey for me. Or if someone attended the appointment with him, turn to that person: I'm curious about what you notice.
Finally, anytime you determine a diagnosis in an assessment, requisite evidence within the assessment will support that diagnostic claim. If you give your client a diagnosis of ADHD, the MSE will include restless, reduced concentration, etc. in support of that diagnosis.

MENTAL STATUS EXAM

DOMAIN	SELECTION
Appearance	see earlier detailed table
Eye contact	see earlier detailed table
Orientation	see earlier detailed table
Alertness	see earlier detailed table
Attitude	see earlier detailed table
Rapport	see earlier detailed table
Behavior	see earlier detailed table
Subjective Mood	see earlier detailed table
Objective Affect	see earlier detailed table
Speech product, not content	see earlier detailed table
Thought Process	see earlier detailed table
Thought Content	see earlier detailed table
Perceptions	see earlier detailed table
Cognition	see earlier detailed table
Insight	see earlier detailed table
Judgement	see earlier detailed table
Intellectual Ability	see earlier detailed table
***SI/HI Risk**	see earlier detailed table DOCUMENT EACH SESSION, **regardless of risk history and even if on telephone**
***Treatment Phase**	see detailed table DOCUMENT EACH SESSION
***Motivation** 1-10, 10 being highest	see detailed table DOCUMENT EACH SESSION

20

TREATMENT PHASE II: ROLE INDUCTION/THERAPEUTIC INFORMED CONSENT

It's been my experience that few of you will pay attention to this section because you want to use your time more wisely – this process requires an investment in time at the start of treatment. Sadly, it's also been my experience that you're going to waste **at least** twice as much time making up for this unwise decision. Even sadder is that you won't link the two together. All part of working in a free capitalist society.

When executed properly, the therapeutic informed consent (TIC, see next page) can result in more streamlined and cohesive treatment with little to no cancellations and no-shows, and a less than one percent recidivism rate. When clients know what to expect and the clinician responds competently and consistently, then treatment tends to flow seamlessly. This is true for all of us. Loosey goosey often lands you in the debit side of the accounting book, especially with recidivism. This is my TIC, tailored to my client base. You must create one for your client base and pass it through your supervisor before you use it. Mine was applauded by The Joint Commission.

SAMPLE

ROLE INDUCTION/THERAPEUTIC INFORMED CONSENT

1. I am ethically obliged to check if you want to hurt/kill yourself or someone else at start of each session and other communications. Life spins on a dime and I see you only 1 of 168 hours/week. Until we complete the "Safety & Recovery Plan", please verbally contract with me your understanding and agreement: You will not hurt/kill yourself or another person, **on purpose or by accident**, before you either see me or speak with me live.
2. Consider resources needed to succeed here - groups, alarm clock, rides, child care.
3. Group work involves learning, practice, and feedback – vital to success with certain skills.
4. Consider therapy goal(s). You change you. Too, it is rare that between two or more people only one person is the "problem". Parents, please be sensitive to the fact that children are like canaries in the mine despite any help they may need.
5. *Happy* and *self-esteem* result from productive living, not treatment goals. What is the behavioral concern? Why is it a concern? How will you use the 167 hours without me to achieve your goals? If I leave, how will you continue uninterrupted with your goals?
6. Behavior is our focus. Your prescriber is concerned with symptoms.
7. Consider that relationships can remain unchanged, improve, or fail because of treatment.
8. Consider me a mirror. I will supportively share what I observe or what I guess without giving advice. To keep us on track, I will raise a finger and say "I'd like to redirect."
9. Consider the power of "I" statements, instead of global and impersonal "you" statements.
10. Consider self-responsibility for your thoughts, feelings, and actions, regardless of what others think or do. If you blame others for your thoughts, feelings, actions or circumstances, then others drive your life. That is a problem only if you do not consciously choose it. *What others think of me is none of my business. If I ask, I will listen non-defensively.*
11. Consider self-responsibility again. If you miss or reschedule 3 sessions, we'll discuss what needs your attention more than this, before we schedule another appointment.

12. Consider commitment to change. Keep appointments when you "don't feel like it", complete homework, be fearless in sessions to be fearless outside of sessions.
13. Consider that I'll always believe you.
14. Consider respect. Self-respect means avoiding excuses for self and others.
15. Consider self-disclosure and feedback, both for your benefit.
16. Consider that the longer we work together, the less productive we may be. Getting "comfortable" has a price. Let's keep it between 8-12 sessions (not etched in stone).
17. Consider why I won't be the first to say "hello" in public.
18. Consider that I will not share your information with ANYONE, excluding professionals, even with your permission. I support YOU in sharing YOUR information.
19. Consider what makes your work effective – our goodbye - which begins the first session.
20. ***By signing below, I acknowledge I read (or had read to me) and understood all the above. I asked for and received clarification to my satisfaction.***

21

TREATMENT PHASE III: SMART INDIVIDUAL SERVICE PLAN

An individualized service plan (ISP) – a specific, measurable (behavioral), achievable (realistic), relevant, and time-bound service plan – SMART -- is essential to treatment. The ISP is the roadmap, regardless of the modality selected. For the those who think client-centered means anything that the client arrives with – wrong. I don't know where you received that information, but no such thing exists outside of chips and dip with friends.

Clients frequently enter treatment with a variety of concerns. Avoid fractured treatment by prioritizing concerns on the ISP to no more than two closely related **behavioral** concerns simultaneously. We don't treat symptoms, prescribers do. There's always a behavior behind any concern. Nope, not listening. This isn't my first rodeo.

Clients cannot productively work on multiple concerns simultaneously. Think through this. I've returned service plans to practitioners that included three concerns above and beyond safety goals. Each session is 50 minutes. How will the client and you meaningfully and continuously address three concerns in 50 minutes? Solution: select the concern most likely to benefit the other two. Discuss this with the client. You're modeling how to solve problems. Prioritize which concern comes first, second, and third. Don't forget to specify that in the ISP clinical note. Now, you're ready to proceed. The intake note will identify all the concerns with the prioritization given to each. The always-present safety plan long-term goal is one of the two long-term goals if DTS/DTO is a primary treatment concern for the client.

Each long-term goal – the discharge goal – is composed of multiple short-term objectives that "end" in achieving or "discharging" the long-term goal.

Each long-term goal's "discharge goal" begins at the start of treatment and is, therefore, addressed regularly. Isn't that lovely?

The ISP always includes a "safety" long-term goal, regardless of the client's safety status. Life spins on a dime. Not everyone who completes suicide or homicide has a history of either

Always include a "vocational" piece. How does the client fill the day and week? This is what builds self-esteem, not talking about it.

Regardless of how challenging ISP development can be, do not complete this for the client. If you're my student, you'd be counting the ethical violations you've just engaged in. Clients don't own ISPs they don't develop. Trash cans do. Solution: Ask questions intended to flesh out client personal goals and objectives. Together, you can easily make them SMART.

NOTE re Diagnosis and ISP

Diagnostic symptoms are not for ISP, they're for the psychiatrist, NP, or PA. Medications target symptoms. We, counselors, target observable behaviors or their absence.

To formulate a comprehensive client picture that guides decisions, the following spheres are necessary:

1. **Primary diagnoses**: Major depressive disorder
2. **Personality diagnoses**: No diagnosis, histrionic features
3. **Medical:** thyroidectomy (takes oral replacement), moderate rheumatoid arthritis
4. **Psychosocial stressors**: divorced 1 year ago, P/T > F/T employment
5. **Global ability to function (GAF)**: at start of service, again at conclusion of service

SAMPLE

INDIVIDUAL SERVICE PLAN

Name: BOOP, Bernard **Date**: 2/21/2043

SMART LTG #1: I will remain safe from suicide for 3 consecutive months.

Baseline (current measure of behavior): SI 2 x week, ER care 2 x week, inpatient 6 x in past yr.

Strengths/supports to progress with this LTG: Community professional and personal supports (crisis center, spouse, best friend). Strategies acquired over course of treatment (mindfulness, thought redirection). Ownership of treatment such that treatment continues uninterrupted. Increased motivation to level 9 of maximum 10, weekly therapy and case management

Potential barriers to progress with this LTG: limited assertion skills, anxiety levels reach to 10 of 10, multiple therapists have resulted in fractured treatment (trust, wellness maintenance issues)

Red required for each service plan, regardless of safety status. Tailor other goals to each client.

Short-Term Goal (SMART)	Intervention(s)	Projected Completion Date	Outcome Completion, Extension (only once), Revision Date
1. Change Personal Safety Plan as things change Baseline: New therapist and my stress has increased from level 8 to 10 of 10	Case management, therapy 1:1 therapy, 2 x week, crisis care prn	Unlike other service plan goals, this goal is permanent and changes as I need it to	Unlike other service plan goals, this goal is permanent and changes as I need it to
2. I will always **SPEAK with you** before acting on SI Baseline: my stress level at 8 of 10 (10 highest)	In person, Phone, Zoom with therapist as needed (prn)	Unlike other service plan goals, this goal is permanent and changes as I need it to	Unlike other service plan goals, this goal is permanent and changes as I need it to
3. I will not suicide on purpose or by accident. Baseline: Passive SI, but my stress level is increasing	Verbal contract, this service plan 1:1 therapy, 2 x week	Unlike other service plan goals, this goal is permanent and changes as I need it to	Unlike other service plan goals, this goal is permanent and changes as I need it to
4. I will create a list of 3 PERSONAL supports Baseline: I feel alone and isolated	1:1 therapy, 2 x week; agency crisis care prn; case mgmt. prn Appt w/ myself at 1PM every day for 15 minutes to reflect on this.	2 March 2043	C: 1 March 2043: Popeye, Mary Poppins, Elmer Fudd

Short-Term Goal (SMART)	Intervention(s)	Projected Completion Date	Outcome Completion, Extension (only once), Revision Date
5. ID 3 relaxation techniques that can be used outside of session at any time Baseline: My techniques are useful when I'm home (television, YouTube)	1:1 therapy, 2 x week, case mgmt. prn, agency crisis care prn	15 March 2043	E to 15 April 2043: ID'ed 2 of 3 relaxation techniques (deep breathing, reality checks)
6. I will turn to one of my supports as needed.	Identified personal support	ongoing	Ongoing until a change is needed

SMART LTG #2: I will not "rage" for 2 consecutive weeks

Baseline (current measure of behavior): I "rage" minimum 2 x day

Strengths/supports for LTG: I don't want to lose my partner, partner says my eyes begin to widen before I rage, motivation for change = 8 of 10 (10 highest), stop using punching bag, calendar to note successes, weekly group and 1:1 therapy and case mgmt, couples therapy as needed

Potential barriers to LTG: uses punching bag that only sustains energy level, resents controlling parents, limited assertion skills, afraid he may have married his parents.

Short-Term Goal (SMART)	Intervention(s)	Projected Completion Date	Outcome Completion, Extension (only once), Revision Date
1. Practice IDing the thought(s) right before I rage Baseline: I see red, my eyes get big	Mindfulness technique, partner will cue mindfulness technique when he sees my eyes open wide. Weekly case management, group & 1:1 therapy	10 March 2043	C: 5 March 2043, but will continue this STG
2. Stop punching bag in garage until it's safe to Baseline: punching bag "releases steam", but increases anger focus	Walk and deep breathe, jog, mindfulness technique, weekly case management, group & 1:1 therapy	immediately	
3. learn to self-disclose Baseline: I don't self-disclose, I rage	Weekly group therapy & 1:1	10 March 2043	
4. Self-disclose to partner twice daily for 2 consecutive weeks. Baseline: I don't self-disclose the hard stuff	Partner, weekly group & 1:1	10 April 2043	
5. Starting today, track learned skills in daily diary for 3 months. Baseline: I don't know how my behavior affects my mood	Personal and partner daily diaries, couples counseling every 2 weeks	10 April 2043	
6. learn to make 1 assertion statement per day Baseline: I rage	Weekly group therapy & 1:1	10 March 2043	

22

TREATMENT PHASE IV: TALK/ PROCESS/AMBIVALENCE/CHANGE

Few have issues with this phase because it's congruent with preconceptions of what THERAPY is – a consequence of accepting the myth of psychotherapy.

Non-Negotiable: Don't provide a therapy, especially *directive therapy* (EMDR, DBT, CBT) if you misunderstand the modality or are unprepared to execute it as intended. It's fine to borrow from a modality, but understand the consequences when you do. I'll explain: If I add a piece of DBT to Gestalt therapy, I can't call it DBT or Gestalt. When clients dislike what you're doing and you're fond of describing every step you take, they're likely to reject DBT and Gestalt therapy when another clinician tries to use it. Humans are like that. I tried it once two years ago. I won't like it. Do you see what happened? You violated an ethical code AND placed the client and another professional in a predicament.

Directive therapies: Thorough adherence to the model is mandatory. Supervision ensures that.

Therapy is **continuously** intersecting phases – from intake to last meeting

1. Clients hold the floor. Keep session on track with redirection

2. Listen, don't talk. If you must, keep it incredibly brief

3. There really is no interest in how good or smart the professional is outside of competence. If as a clinician, you have a need to be recognized, address this in supervision or personal therapy.

4. Never advise unless it's balanced so client genuinely chooses

THERAPY PHASE	DESCRIBED
Basic Skill Steps	NO short-cuts, housekeeping always at top of hour
Step 1: Mutual Ethics, Mutual Respect & Competence, Wellness & Boundaries	-Agency Informed Consent, Therapeutic Informed Consent (TIC) -What to expect (you, counseling, redirection, note taking, culture, personal needs & idiosyncrasies) -Role Induction (TIC) -Natural Consequences (TIC)
Step 2: Attend, Empathize, minimize your talk and questions **Step 1**: Working alliance**Step 2**: Story & strengths **Step 3**: Goals **Step 4**: Re-story **Step 5**: Action	Culturally & individually appropriate visuals (eye contact), vocal qualities, non/verbal tracking skills Convert questions into statements to keep the flow of conversation instead of witness-attorney examination
Step 3: Essential Listening & Data Gathering Sequence	1st Observe 2nd Question: Open, Closed, Clarify, convert into statements to avoid attorney-witness problem 3rd Encourage, Summarize once and only before first half hour 4th Reflect meaning & affect – no more than twice in the first half hour to avoid alienating client
Step 4: Interview Structure	Complete interview – listen, attend with all senses Evaluate interview for accuracy and understanding 1: Establish a healthy **working** alliance 2: listen for story, strengths (resources), limitations 3: Goals 4: Typically, story organically changes after first as client grows more comfortable and relies on your redirection skills. 5: Action plan
Step 5: Focus	
Step 6: Empathically Clarify/ Confront	

THERAPY PHASE	DESCRIBED
Step 7: 1-2 content and affect reflections, interpret/reframe, summary	Reflect content and affect: Reframe: Summary: Only once and before first half of session. **Clients summarize because:** **1.We know change is more likely when we hear ourselves talking about it or aspects of it** **2.Focus remains on client, not us or how well we remember the session** **3.Alerts us re client inner workings and what "stuck" this session and the next session when the client begins with a summary of this session.**
Step 8: Self-Disclosure and Feedback	
Step 9: Change: Action Strategies	ID +/- Logical Consequences Instruction/Psychoeducation --- Distress tolerance - Mindfulness re concern and its generalizability --- Acceptance for human infallibility, you'll do it again --- Thought Regulation to ensure emotion regulation
Step 10: Theoretical skill integration	Fidelity to theory that fits client and client need(s) best Integrate skills: practice, solicit feedback and increase comfort with mistakes, practice, more feedback and more mistakes, practice
Step 11: Find professional self – style, voice, first theory	
Clinical assessment phase	Continuously updated, with a minimum of an annual review or in cases of hospitalization. This is the framework of THERAPY. This phase, the most informative, provides data vital to understanding the client's history and current position in the world. This phase underscores behavioral dynamics and trends for client, family of origin, and supports. The information can and often changes as details emerge during other phases. This phase includes reason for treatment, past treatment, family history, social and vocational history, substance use, medical conditions, etc. *When clients take psychotropic medication, this phase typically includes a psychiatric evaluation alongside an informative document for what it does and does not contain.*

THERAPY PHASE	DESCRIBED
Role induction/therapeutic informed consent phase	These are the basic guidelines that structure THERAPY delivery. It limits confusion/disagreement across the lifespan of the therapeutic alliance, and is referenced as needed. Tailored to client comprehension level.
ISP Phase, which includes discharge planning	A living, breathing, SMART document that reflects where the client is at any given moment. The most difficult for practitioners. The ISP structures the talking/processing phase and informs the other phases. For some practitioners, it is not as sexy as the talk/process phase. Practitioners tend not to invest the necessary time here. Short-term goals not achieved within a realistic time frame will be modified or removed from the SMART ISP. Thus, the ISP is an ever-evolving road map reflecting where THERAPY was and where THERAPY is headed. Without it, the talking/processing phase lacks structure, is lengthy, and is often duplicated. A dramatic example of this is a client's 7 jumbo-sized charts about the same concern across six years and four practitioners. In community mental health and insurance-driven treatment, it is the cornerstone of billing. When clinical notes are unlinked from the ISP, payors can deny payment. Enough denials can result in significant financial sanctions and allegations of fraud. Enough financial sanctions result in layoffs. Layoffs can result in clinic closures. Make no mistake, THERAPY is a financial and legal business.
Talking/Processing phase	Encapsulates, condenses, and articulates the previous phases via specific clinical skills. THERAPY time is condensed time, since time is of the essence – after ~12 sessions, effectiveness declines. THERAPY is conversational but is not a social conversation. The goals and specific clinical skills and modalities are responsible for this. In this phase, the practitioner relies heavily on data collected from other phases to assist the client in creating change where it was not previously possible.
Future pacing phase	
All together and over again	1. THERAPY phases recycle with the addition of new data to any phase. When one phase changes, the others will.

NICE ≠ WARM OR SUPPORTIVE

"Nice" is for friends. Nice doesn't serve clients. Nice brought the client to you. **Don't suffer from nice**.

Strategic application of clinical skills is key, not mainstream sociability. Clients seek us for assistance with fundamental change or to discover they're not yet "ripe" for change. Both are equally reasonable and "right".

SAFE ≠ COMFORTABLE

Change isn't comfortable, which is why clinical settings must be safe.

Clinical Assertion + Modality Adherence ▶ THERAPEUTIC conversation,
not SOCIAL conversation = CHANGE

AMBIVALENCE

As we work with clients, especially at the start, we're alert to ambivalence. Ambivalence can influence motivation for change.

We're tasked to assess and assist. I'm not referencing truth and lies. The search for truth is an open invitation to lock horns. I'm not the police and am not interested in "catching" anything. That said, I don't ignore incongruent statements. I'm interested in the client's world, which makes lingual, paralingual, and unconscious inconsistencies are explored for change to occur. I want to understand. What am I talking about? Here's an example:

Client's lips: *I want to save my marriage.*

Client's feet: Missed appointments, forgets out-of-session work, minimal engagement

If I'm competent, I see the discrepancy between word and action. If I ignore it thinking more of the same will help, it's likely everyone in that room will be disappointed. Nor do I leap on it with a clinical got you. My job to assess and assist. How, oh how, do I proceed when someone demonstrates ambivalence or low motivation? I will ***temporarily*** interrupt my current modality - for example, Gestalt - for a set of basic clinical skills that will target ambivalence/ motivation. Once the client achieves greater clarity, I revert to Gestalt or therapy stops. To learn how to do all this, I will register for the course where I can learn to apply basic pre-existing clinical skills to resolve the ambivalence/motivation question.

In my experience, it takes approximately one to two sessions to resolve the ambivalence/motivation question: the client and I stop therapy or we press on with the original modality – Gestalt.

Session 1 or 2, Gestalt → note ambivalence → stop Gestalt, apply basic skills →

motivation increases/client realizes unreadiness for change → return to Gestalt

23

TREATMENT PHASE V: FUNCTIONAL ASSESSMENT & CASE CONCEPTUALIZATION

Functional Assessment

Many functional assessment tools have come and gone in efforts to facilitate appropriate levels of care. To organize your thinking, below is a composite of ranges from superior function to no function. Select the function level that best fits the client with an "X". Now, provide a score 1-10, 10 being highest function for that level. This information – don't copy/paste – helps inform the intake clinical note and case conceptualization presented during supervision.

1-10		SELECT HIGHEST FUNCTION
		Superior function in a wide range of activities, problems are managed, is sought out by others due to positive personal qualities. No symptoms.
		Absent or minimal symptoms (e.g., mild anxiety before an exam), good function in all domains, interested and involved in a wide range of activities, socially successful, generally satisfied with life, no more than everyday problems or concerns (e.g. an occasional argument with family members).

1-10		SELECT HIGHEST FUNCTION
7	X	If symptoms are present, they are transient and natural reactions to psychosocial stressors (e.g., difficulty concentrating after family argument); no more than slight social, occupational or academic difficulty, temporarily failing behind in schoolwork).
		Mild symptoms (e.g., depressed mood and mild insomnia) OR some social, occupational, or academic difficulties (e.g., occasional truancy, theft within household), generally functions well, has some meaningful interpersonal relationships.
		Moderate symptoms (e.g., flat affect, circumstantial speech, occasional panic attacks) OR moderate social, occupational, or academic difficulties (e.g., few friends, peer or co-worker conflict).
		Serious symptoms (e.g., suicidal ideation, severe obsessional rituals, frequent shoplifting) OR serious social, occupational, or academic impairment (e.g., no friends, does not retain employment).
		Some impaired reality testing or communication (e.g., speech at times illogical, obscure, or irrelevant) OR major impairment in several domains (e.g., work, school, family relations, judgment, thinking, or mood [e.g., depressed man avoids friends, neglects family, unable to work; child frequently aggressive toward younger children, defiant at home, fails academically]).
		Behavior considerably influenced by delusions or hallucinations OR seriously impaired communication or judgment (e.g., sometimes incoherent, largely inappropriate behavior, suicidal preoccupation) OR does not function in nearly all domains (e.g., in bed all day, no work, no home or friends).
		Some danger of hurting self or others (e.g., suicide attempts without clear expectation of death; frequently violent; manic excitement) OR occasionally fails to maintain minimal personal hygiene OR gross communication impairment (e.g., incoherent or mute).
		Persistent danger of hurting self or others (e.g., recurrent violence) OR persistently does not maintain minimal personal hygiene OR serious suicidal acts with clear intent of death.
		Unable to function OR inadequate information

Case Conceptualization

For meaningful supervisor and peer insights, use the format below to present new or challenging cases. The details provide a clear clinical profile of your client.

Oral Presentation Only: seek peer suggestions for current issues or concerns in work with client, future work with the client or other clients. Give peers an outline, not all information that you would in a written conceptualization.

STEP	STEP DETAIL
Summary introduction of client background	Bulk of data from Intake Assessment can change during next few sessions a. Brief description (age, gender, ethnicity, place of residence, education, vocation, financial resources, diagnoses [standing and rule-outs], functional level, medication, services received) b. Family and support network: marital status, children, family of origin (background, frequency of contact), community support (church, clubs). c. Environment: unique resources, barriers and facilitators to success, life events, stressors. d. Vocational history: history, work skills and training, hobbies, employability, job readiness, vocational interests (interview and test data). e. Previous service provision: successes and difficulties. f. Personal factors: view of work, coping skills, personal styles, life experiences, and costs/benefits to working.
Presenting concern(s)	a. Summarize diagnosis, present and previous treatment, hospitalizations, medications, etc. b. Summarize current function level (e.g., housing, ADLs, living skills, transportation). c. Summarize social situation; financial position; identify significant others, their understanding of the client's condition and prognosis, their contribution to recovery. Does the client view them as supportive of the rehabilitation process? d. Any incentives or disincentives to work or program participation? e. Summarize medical issues
Agency/Clinic Contact	a. Identify client's reason for referral, "why now?", treatment goals b. Summarize current treatment program 4. Focus of contact (Describe your relationship with the client to date) a. Identify goals you have developed with the client., and any desired outcomes. b. Intervention plan to help achieve these goals (specific, measurable, time-limited). c. Current progress in intervention plan, and prognosis for treatment. d. Plan for terminating services.

STEP	STEP DETAIL
Focus of Contact with the Client	a. Describe to-date work with the client. b. Identify client-developed goals, and status of those goals. c. Describe and rationalize the theoretical approach(es) used and the outcome(s). d. Describe and rationalize treatment interventions and strategies used and the outcome(s). e. Describe rationale for completed assessments and screenings, discuss results, impact on work with client. f. Discuss relevant multicultural issues or considerations that impact the client's life. g. Discuss current issues or concerns in your work with the client.
Summary	Provide a summary of the client's current situation including an assessment of progress and prognosis for treatment, as you move toward termination.

24

TREATMENT PHASE VI: MORE CASE CONCEPTUALIZATION & SERVICE PLANNING

Objectives

Understand the role of case conceptualization in your primary treatment methodology. Skills include

a) Assess client behavioral concerns. Remember, we don't treat symptoms. Prescribers do that. ID behaviors to be reduced/eliminated or behaviors to begin

b) Co-develop a SMART plan of action

c) ID treatment supports and obstacles, ID what can mitigate obstacles

A **trigger** is an event preceding a behavior, one that increase or decrease the behavior. Triggers -- affective, somatic, behavioral, cognitive -- can trigger emotional and physiological responses, and are subject to contextual and relational factors.

Behavior is a thought, emotion, or action in response to a trigger. Short-term and long-term consequences of the behavior cause the client to continue or discontinue a behavior. Each behavior could potentially have affective, somatic, behavioral, and cognitive components.

Positive consequences increase the chances a behavior is repeated through a pleasant experience or the absence of a negative one – no bathroom duty. **Negative consequences** decrease the chances a behavior is repeated by a negative experience - being reprimanded - or the absence of something desired - I sleep on the couch instead of next to my partner). Humans tend to repeat behaviors that provide something positive or remove something negative. So. (a) ID consequences and (b) collaborate with the client to explore all components of each consequence.

EX: A client who reports cocaine use – **behavior** - may feel anxious when alone at home at night - **contextual antecedent** - or connected when around family - **relational antecedent**. Or client may feel depressed thinking, "I will always be alone" - **cognitive antecedent**.

So, remembering that thoughts trigger emotions, which trigger behavior, ID antecedents by pinpointing conditions that affect behavior

Cognitive: ID one typical thought just before X.

Affective: Tell me what you felt right before you did X.

Behavior: I'm interested in what you're doing right before X.

Somatic: Describe how do you feel physically before X happens ... (nauseous, for example).

Contextual: Tell me where and when X usually happens.

Relational: I'm curious if you X with everyone, or just certain people.

Cognitive: The first thought after X happened was...

Affective: Describe how you felt immediately after X.

Behavioral: Share how you behaved after X

Somatic: Describe the physical sensations after X (trembling, for example)

Contextual: I'm curious if you ended up in a different location by the time X ended

Relational: Again, I'm curious about which people make X more likely to happen and which less likely to happen. Because ....

During a functional assessment, short-term consequences (STC) and long-term consequences (LTC) are assessed. STCs reinforce behaviors, while LTCs tend to be negative outcomes. The STC of cocaine use is intoxication or escape from something. The LTC of cocaine use is legal, familial, or physical problems.

I hope you're thinking to yourself – It's a good idea to know the positive and negative consequences of behaviors if I'm going to focus the timing and service. Bravo. For example, the intervention follows a negative trigger to offset the negativity the trigger elicited. What does the client hope to avoid? To know that is to help the client potentially decrease the need for cocaine.

More requests for information to illuminate STC:

> *Tell me about the kind of attention you get from X.*
>
> *Describe at least two benefits of X.*
>
> *Describe what X helps you avoid.*
>
> *Describe the 'rush' you get from X.*

All this assumes a thorough understanding of how to gather information while establishing rapport. That is easy to say, but difficult to achieve for three reasons:

1. Most professionals ask too many questions, which creates passive and bored clients
2. Most professionals talk too much, which increases client absences and withdrawals
3. Most professionals are invested in looking smart, which makes them believe they have the answers to client problems

What's a professional to do? In the foreword to this book I mentioned two Hollywood characters that helped me be professional while being myself. You'll think I'm kidding, but I'm not: Mr. Falk's rumpled and *brilliantly curious* lieutenant Columbo neither sidesteps the process nor struggles with the perpetrator. On the other end of the spectrum stands Mr. Eastwood's inspector Callahan whose *parsimonious* verbalizations communicate volumes. Columbo never locks horns with the criminal any more than Callahan resorts to self-promotion or speeches. Columbo simply moves forward, consistently himself, applying his professional skills. Although Callahan skirts procedure, his transparency and focus without speeches are what make him, and Columbo, my perfect models. True, today's students don't recognize either character when I discuss them. They can stream them anytime, anywhere once they've digested the text and lectures.

A question for you – what did you notice about the content of the four (4) gray boxes directly above? I hope you noticed I didn't ask a single question.

I dislike questions for two (2) reasons. One, they reinforce the false belief that I'm in charge. I'm in charge of staying on track and following the service plan, but clients own the floor. Not a single client ever changed anything by listening to me ask questions or "share important information". The truth is questions create passive clients and establish a courtroom setting of questions and answers. So, I do everything I can to convert questions into statements that keep the conversation moving forward. If you don't believe me, record your next session and listen carefully to the client's tone and length of sentences after you stop talking. Unless the client is someone who will talk to an empty chair, you'll hear a difference. It always begins with a somewhat flat "Yeah."

Anyway, all that leads us to case conceptualization.

Case conceptualization is the structured process of gathering, understanding, and interpreting a client's presenting concerns as anchored in individual history, personality, and current circumstances. It is a structured summary of findings that "maps" treatment: precipitating events, protective factors, predisposing factors, perpetuating factors, prognosis, treatment plan, and progress. There are several steps:

STEP	STEP DETAIL
Case Conceptualization	1. An objective, focused, and informed framework for understanding clients 2. The roadmap for effective treatment interventions and techniques that assess and provide opportunities for change 3. Foundational to client change measurement 4. Facilitates rapport, client hope, and burn-out 5. Avoids problems that distract clinician and client from core goals
When to Case Conceptualize? (Indications/ Contraindications)	1. Starts the first session with increasing refinement as treatment progresses 2. First session assesses and lists current difficulties 3. Contributes to SMART treatment plan development. If done earlier than session 1 or 2, treatment planning may require modification in response to emergent information 4. SMART treatment plans are living and breathing and are routinely revisited for "fit"

STEP	STEP DETAIL
Step 1/3 How to Case Conceptualize: Assess client concerns	1. Use client self-report 2. Determine baseline function, goals, and progress. Frequently highlight important improvements and/or continuing symptoms. Information obtained from self-report can increase insight into how clients think and behave and important needs. 3. Use psychological, social, occupational, and financial problem lists to ID difficulties during first part of session 1 (5-10). Use open-ended questions ("What brings you in today?" "What issues would you like to focus on?"). Problems best described in terms of --- frequency - How often does the symptom occur? - AND --- intensity - How mild or severe is it? - AND --- functional impact - use numbers to describe the influence problems have on function. Some clients describe difficulties or goals in vague or abstract ways ("I want to improve my life", "I want to be happy again.") ** table below 4. Assess cognition. EX: in CBT, it is helpful to examine client thoughts as perceived by client. A common and structured approach is to ask questions related to how the client perceives him/herself, others, and the future. A client may describe himself as incapable or a burden. He may view others as critical or hard to please. To him, the future is pessimistic with pending losses and disappointments. 5. Assess behaviors and precipitating events. Precipitating events are also thoughts, emotions, behaviors that activate, trigger, or compound difficulties. Track triggers, behavior, and consequences per *** template. The template, a functional assessment, is predicated on the assumption that triggers and consequences shape behavior.

STEP	STEP DETAIL
Step 2/3 How to Case Conceptualize: Clinical Hypotheses and Service Plan	Step 1 info is needed here for intervention options and treatment techniques, which often change as new information emerges during treatment. Reflect content to enhance communication and trust... EX: Since retirement, you've experienced many life transitions and losses. Prior positive and ambitious thoughts are now negative and pessimistic. You seem fearful of the future. As a result, you've reduced your activities and have withdrawn from family and friends. The outcome of case conceptualization is a SMART service plan that provides clear direction. The *co-created* SMART service plan includes causes of current difficulties - cognitive and behavioral factors. EX: So far, you've IDed thoughts and behaviors that may contribute to your difficulties. Self-perception and your view of the future are negative, and you've stopped previously pleasurable activities. Some considerations: (a) let's explore your thoughts for a more balanced view of current difficulties. (b) let's explore re-engaging in pleasurable activities. Thoughts?
Step 3/3 How to Case Conceptualize: Future Pacing	Clients often simply agree with clinician recommendations. A reason to ID potential obstacles to treatment early - avoid or minimize setbacks or failures, although those can be integral to meaningful change. Collaborating with clients reduces over-compliance (passivity), increases "active" engagement, and generalization to other life issues. Future pacing allows clients to ID potential barriers to progress, particularly as they near the end. Some are logistic difficulties (financial, travel), personal beliefs (concerns about stigma, effectiveness of treatment) or interpersonal issues (family not supportive of therapy). To provide competent services is to provide services that extrapolate knowledge - minimize future returns to the service provider that could have been easily addressed with this skill. Life happens. Discuss how it does.

STEP	STEP DETAIL
Case Conceptualization in Brief Therapy	Brief therapy case conceptualization differs from longer treatment: o No time for case formulation delays o Account for time limitations in treatment and SMART goals o Treatment focus limits the depth of cognitive interventions. EX: While addressing automatic thoughts and intermediate beliefs as foci of treatment is frequent, addressing core beliefs is more difficult. If core beliefs are addressed, this typically occurs indirectly through surface-level techniques or at a time when the client is ready for such work.

** **How to Case Conceptualize: Assess client concerns:** Problems and subsequent goals are best described in specific terms to maintain clinical focus.

CONCERN	FREQUENCY	SUBJECTIVE SEVERITY	BEHAVIORAL IMPACT
Social isolation	Home 6 of 7 days	High Moderate	Distressing; socially debilitating; estranged from family /friends
Feelings of worthlessness	Almost constantly	Intense when present, severe	Highly distressing. Influences ability to function at work, social, intimate relationships
Anger outbursts	3 x week	High	Highly distressing. Influences social, intimate relationships

*** **How to Case Conceptualize: Assess client concerns**

Trigger	Specific Observable Behavior	Short-Term Consequence (1 second or and 1 hour post-behavior)	Long-Term Consequence (lasting results)

25

TREATMENT PHASE VII: FUTURE PACING

Future pacing is a technique I use, typically just before we begin reducing the number of visits, to help clients imagine future success and barriers to success. At that point, the client is better armed to face challenges. A word about future pacing and service titration: The client can express readiness to complete and stop attending session. Always. But that isn't what drives titration and completion. You're the professional on board. Do you agree with the client? If not, what's your plan?

Realistic barriers are especially important since they derail change in the moment and later. I ask clients to imagine a scenario when the problematic behavior is triggered, what are the specific circumstances, what are the first thoughts, what emotions do thoughts stir, what are the **specific** steps and/or resources that would – not could -- resolve those scenarios, what would not. Don't release specificity. The client will be tempted. More importantly, you'll be tempted. Clients who hear themselves proactively addressing change in their lives are more likely to succeed. The words and imagery are integral to links between change and resources, available and needed. Moreover, I introduce observations of client behavior such as increased breathing and swallowing, licking lips, anything that will "round out" the exercise.

26

TREATMENT PHASE VIII: TRANSFER, COMPLETION, CLOSURE WITHDRAWAL & CLOSURE

Transfer

ETHICAL REASON TO TRANSFER	QUESTIONABLE REASONS
Current clinician leaving	Lack of skills – supervision is for this. As graduate students, we had no skills but practiced due to supervision.
Conflict of interest	Manipulation of client to reject service
Client refuses to work with clinician	Method to contain caseload size and types of concerns
Dual relationship	Doesn't like a particular population – successful mostly in private practice
Conscientious objection re transference, countertransference: Clinician's struggle with similar concern as client	Discriminatory beliefs
Current clinician leaving	
Supervision unavailable for specific concern while clinician acquires skills	
Caseload number and diagnoses unmanageable	

When transferring a client, thoroughly debrief the next clinician in writing at a minimum. Although non-billable, case notations reflect these actions. That has positive implications.

1. It allows a potential last session that includes the exit-ing and entering clinicians.
2. It ensures client treatment continues as seamlessly as possible.
3. It ensures accurate transfer of case data from one clinician to the other.
4. ** Always have two methods to ensure the above for continued client safety and progress.

SITUATION	RESPONSE
No contact	When closing due to no contact, it's important to reach out to the client a minimum of three (3) times. All three efforts differ and are separated by nothing less than 3 business days. That means, at a minimum, outreach must extend across nine (9) business days before I close a chart. 1. Telephone call and message 2. email 3. text 4. letter In cases of clients with a history of DTS/DTO, request a police wellness check. If your agency or city has a mobile emergency team, contact them. Charting, regardless of risk, is succinct, specific, clear, and includes supervisors. Separate note for each separate act or person consulted with.

SITUATION	RESPONSE
Cancellation and/or No Show	If you don't engage the TIC during the first session, you'll struggle with cancellations and no shows. Although, suffering from nice leaves clients bored and unmotivated, sessions that don't stimulate action, clinician timidity, and other reasons. First, clients often have lives where many things happen at once. When they cancel/no show for more than three times we discuss it as I said we would in the TIC. Pay close attention to my word choice and tone. *Anna, the first time we met we discussed absences. It's okay. Don't worry. If you look at this, you'll see you've missed three sessions in the last two and half months. I know a lot is happening and it's clearly important. That's why I'd like us to figure out how to manage it so you can feel good about your choices.* Second, the above places Anna in control of her life and her therapy. Missing therapy is not a personal jab at me. It represents other systems and dynamics. When a client misses, it's important to support what's taking them away so its resolution will return them, if they need to return at all. Anna did return as life demands eased. I can dress this up any way I like but, outside of mandated treatment, therapy is really a luxury. The importance of my job to me will never be matched by clients.
Completion	Clients are always free to express readiness to complete and stop attending. But that isn't what drives titration and completion. Do you professionally agree with the client? If you professionally disagree, what's your plan? You must have one. If you professionally agree, do clinical notes support that readiness?
Withdrawal	Sometimes, we know why clients withdraw. In such cases, we assist with a healthy withdrawal, not coercion or manipulation. I solicit input on what could have been different. That's also a creative way to see if I've played a part since soliciting client feedback rarely yields constructive feedback. I tell them I hope to see them again in the future. In cases where there's potential for psychiatric or legal incarceration, I gently state I don't want to see the client hurt, does the client understands the consequences? If the client replies in the affirmative, I verify with: *And they are...*
Timing	Open cases tick, tock, tick, tock. Remember that life spins on a dime? Just because a client denied DTS/DTO the last 10 sessions doesn't remove DTS/DTO from the table. This week, a student learned that. Timing, supported by agency protocol, structure our work. Don't leave cases open unnecessarily. The tick can explode.

SAMPLE

CLOSURE SUMMARY

D/C Date: 02/13/2050 **Intake Date:** 12/01/2049

Client: BOOP, Betty **DOB**: 01/01/2000

Format: In-Person, TLH 1:1 **Total Scheduled Sessions**: 18

Clt Cancel/Reschedule Sessions: 9 **Clinician Cancel Session:** 1

Client Completed Sessions: 8

Reason for Closure

Client will transfer care to physician and student-in-training period has concluded

Primary Concern(s)

-SI (started 3 mo ago), denies DTS/DTO

-American who left Argentina due to end of romantic relationship 3 months prior

-Isolation, lack of independent transportation

-Resides with mother (strained relationship) and grandmother w/ Alzheimer's

-Hypersomnia

-Reduced motivation for daily or professional activities

-Pain (9 to 10, 10 greatest pain)

-Potential opioid abuse or dependency for pain management (prescriber intends to discontinue med, recommended inpatient detox).

MSE	AT INTAKE	AT CLOSURE
Appearance	w/i std limits	w/i std limits
Eye Contact	good	good
Attitude & Rapport	Open yet purposely vague at times	open, interactive, negative, defensive
Behavior	sluggish	Aggressive language
Subjective mood	Depressed, overwhelmed, stressed	Depressed, anxious, agitated
Objective mood	Congruent w/ client report, labile	angry, anxious, determined
Speech	fluent, hyper-expressive, fast not pressured	fluent, quiet, hyper-expressive, fast not pressured
Thought process	Logical, perseverative (opioid med)	loose associations, but within standard limits overall
Thought content	"I can't live without opioids… living with pain is worse than death", life is meaningless because he is unproductive	obsessive, overvalued ideas re own knowledge base re opioids and medical treatment options
Perceptions	"no one loves me because of my disability… they are annoyed because I'm depressed… no one understands me… American medical community is uncaring"	"American doctors never care about patients. They never listen to their patients, no one understands me"
Cognition	alert, focused, attentive	alert, focused, attentive, negative, perseverative
Insight	low	low, especially re opioid
Judgment	reasoned yet impaired as related to opioid	reasoned, over-valued
Intellectual ability	Above average	Above average
SI*	Confirmed for past 3 months, no intent. Used safety plan.	Confirmed, w/o intent. Used safety plan.
HI*	denied	denied
Para-suicidality*	Denied, no evidence	Denied, no evidence
Change phase	Pre-contemplative to contemplative	Pre-contemplative

INTAKE

Psychiatric Diagnosis (trauma; substance use, abuse, dependence [substance, 1st & last use dates, amount, frequency]): Bipolar II (no data re initial dx date), denied trauma

Psychiatric Medication(s): Buspirone for anxiety (45mg q d), denied for bipolar condition

Psychosocial Stressors: isolation, "unproductive", financial challenges, maternal relationship, grandmother (has dementia), lacks close friendships, paternal grandparents assist with transportation.

Medical (specify, dates): Complex Regional Pain Syndrome (CRPS)

Medical Medication (specify type, dosage):

--THC 5mg (~ 3x week, unable to disclose amount)

--fentanyl (75mg/hour, changes patch q 72 hours)

--oxycodone (10mg bid, 3-4 times when pain increases) for CRPS pain (no specific prescriber instructions)

Developmental: denied, no evidence

Social/Interpersonal: Break-up in Argentina 3 months ago after 4 years w/ partner. Left close friends through partner, pets (rats). Distant relationship w/ Mom and maternal grandmother, can be stressful -- mom can be intrusive. No contact with bio-father, but close w/ supportive paternal grandparents -- emotionally, daily activity, transport. 1-2 current online gaming friends, not "close".

Educational/Occupational (specify, dates): computer science BA, unknown graduation date; employed in field for undetermined few years. Stopped due to medical disability

Legal (specify, outcome, dates): denied, no evidence

Personal and Interpersonal Strengths that Facilitated Treatment: Advanced reading, writing, investigative skills. Reaches out to hotline or writer for SI.

Family/Marriage Supports (specify length of relationships): Separated parents. Client resides with Mom and maternal grandmother diagnosed w/ Alzheimer's. No contact w/ father, although close with paternal grandparents -- provide emotional/physical support, transportation. No siblings.

Family Psychiatric (specify person, type, outcome): Maternal grandmother -- Alzheimer's

Additional Relevant Information: N/A

DISCHARGE

Psychiatric Diagnosis (include trauma; substance use, abuse, dependence [substance, 1st & last use dates, amount, frequency]): Bipolar II (no data re initial dx date), Opioid dependence

Psychiatric Medication(s): Buspirone for anxiety (45mg q d), denied for Bipolar condition and no evidence

Psychosocial Stressors: unchanged > isolation, "unproductive", financial challenges, maternal relationship, grandmother w/ dementia, no close friendships, paternal grandparents assist with transportation.

Medical (specify, dates): CRPS

Medical Medication(specify type, dosages): THC 5mg (~ 3x week, unknown amount)

--fentanyl (75mg/hour, changes patch q 72 hours)

--oxycodone (10mg bid, 3-4 times when pain increases) for CRPS pain (no specific prescriber instructions provided, prescriber will terminate script; client found a Phx prescriber willing to prescribe)

Developmental: denied, no evidence

Social/Interpersonal: Romantic break-up in Argentina 3 months ago after 4 years. Left close friends through ex-girlfriend, pets (snakes). Relationship w/ Mom and maternal grandmother not close and was stressful (mom "intrusive"). Lacked close contact with bio-father, but close w/ paternal grandparents who were supportive (emotionally, daily activity, transport). 1-2 current friends described as "not very close", many online gaming friends.

***Educational/Occupational (specify, dates)*:** computer science BA (unknown graduation date); employed in field for undetermined few years. Stopped due to medical disability. Reported desire to resume employment but has not initiated steps.

***Legal (specify, outcome, dates)*:** denied and no evidence

***Personal and Interpersonal Strengths that Facilitated Treatment*:** Communicated in timely manner to reschedule counseling sessions. Timely arrival to sessions. Completed 85% of assignments (journaled feelings about life and relationship loss). Advanced reading, writing, investigative skills. Accessed hotline and writer for SI.

Family/Marriage Supports (specify length of relationships): Separated parents. Client resides with Mom and maternal grandmother who is diagnosed w/ Alzheimer's (stressful for client). No close contact w/ father, although close with paternal grandparents (provide emotional/physical support, transportation). No siblings.

Family Psychiatric (specify person, type, outcome): Maternal grandmother diagnosed w/ Alzheimer's.

Additional Relevant Information: Limitations: CRPS pain from working on assignments or counseling sessions. Met DSM criteria for opioid dependency, mistrusted effectiveness of counseling or pain management offered by physicians other than opioids. Following an extensive search, client located a resource in Phoenix - pain specialist will prescribe fentanyl in conjunction with infusion therapy.

SERVICES PROVIDED (Start/End dates, Frequency, Outcomes)

--1 clinical session/week for 2 weeks >> 2 sessions/week due to SI. Clt kept most appts, but little progress due to commitment to finding another opioid prescriber.

--Declined group therapy and psyched group

--Agency care management, prn

--Inconsistent journaling, writing homework

Course of Treatment

Progress

Client requested services for multiple losses -- romantic relationship, friends, medical care, pets. Intake phase was contemplative, but became pre-contemplative aeb fixed desire only for opioid treatment, not other concerns per intake. Inability to gain opioid exacerbated SI, which necessitated increased weekly sessions -- 2/week. ISP revised to address self-efficacy via journaling, strength-based interventions. Client found Phx MD willing to prescribe opioid pain management.

Limitation to Progress

Client stated CRPS restricted counseling session attendance/homework completion. Opioid dependence aeb: increased doses and tolerance; inability to reduce dosage; much time in pursuit of med -- prescriber discontinued med w/ inpatient detox recommendation; reported inability to live w/o med; failure to fulfill primary social, personal, professional roles; pursued med despite knowledge re habituation and prescriber cautions. Denied use of recommended alternative pain management interventions unique to CRPS. Motivation for change decreased during treatment (contemplation > pre-contemplation). Clt will work only with MDs who prescribe opioids. Declines opioid detox or physical therapy w/o opioids. MDs who do not prescribe opioids are "uncaring, inhumane".

Transition Plan (Client and clinician actions to facilitate care transition)

1. Clinician will prepare clinical record for client transition, esp. if for outside agency.

2. Clinician will present discharge during clinical supervision.

3. Clinician will alert the interdisciplinary team member - opioid prescriber -- who discontinued med.

4. Client will make appt w/ assigned Care Manager during next week.

27

RELEASE OF INFORMATION

A release of information (ROI) is legally necessary before any document exchange of information about a client is provided *to the client*, client family member, or anyone outside the agency that delivers services. This includes verbal exchanges about the client. No ROI? Unsure if there is an ROI, don't give information but do listen and/or take a message –

I can neither confirm nor deny the existence of such a person, but I can listen to what you have to say and take a message [don't say to whom you will give the message].

Note there are to exceptions to the above:

1. medical emergency
2. if *you* call adult or child protective services to report an incident

Prior to the advancement of the portable and electronic health record, medical emergency calls to clinics occurred more frequently. Even so, it's important to know how to legally manage such calls without breaching client confidentiality. If someone rings your clinic requesting information because of a medical emergency, **respond according to your agency's protocol**.

My protocol below may differ from your agency's protocol. **It's your responsibility to verify your agency's protocol in such circumstances.**

1. I request

    a. caller's full name and title

    b. caller's organization name: Typically, a hospital and typically provided at the start of the conversation. Train yourself to listen accurately to all calls that come in.

    c. department caller is calling from: often this is the ER, which is recognizable unless it's in another city, state, country

    d. information requested. In medical emergencies, the only priority is the medication log. Anything else can be managed without documentation, including diagnoses.

    e. **NEVER USE ANY TELEPHONE NUMBERS CALLERS PROVIDE.** If the call is fraudulent, what value does it have?

2. I ensure the caller understands I will look up the number and ring the caller back at that specific department. I will not be deterred from this.

3. I move fast but methodically, someone's welfare is at stake

    a. Immediately, I ask someone to contact the assigned clinician. This is useful if the call is outside my city. Clinicians often know when clients travel.

    b. Immediately, I ask someone to alert a supervisor.

    c. Immediately, I locate the medication log that I MAY or MAY NOT use.

    d. Immediately, find the agency telephone number.

4. I ring the hospital and ask for the specific department and specific individual.

5. If the person that initially rang responds to the call, I have the law on my side. I've taken all reasonable precautions to protect client confidentiality during a crisis.

6. If no one knows that person, I need my supervisor or a proxy.

This business can be tricky; and, because most days are quiet, we're lulled into a belief that things are always quiet. Until they're not.

Back to the ROI itself. Clients must consent to provide themselves and others with all or some of the records. However. The ROI alone is insufficient. An ROI is a process focused on the release of protected client information to other persons, groups, and organizations. Patient information disclosure, however, is not a task to be taken lightly, but not because of purely authoritative reasons.

All that is complicated by several factors, not the least being the age of the information and its trustworthiness. These factors are important because data from height and weight to any assessment falls within the ROI's purview. With this comes responsibility. The service provider as well as the client have a responsibility to ensure the accuracy of the protected information.

RELEASE	DESCRIBED
Unauthorized	Doesn't require client consent. This can happen when a client cannot provide essential information, especially as related to emergency treatment (see discussion above). In such cases, only the information needed to extend life is transferred. If a client has overdosed, the emergency room is entitled to know all the medications on the client's medication log, not treatment progress or diagnoses.
Authorized	Requires client consent. In the case of children, typically both parents, unless once has legally lost custody, or legally authorized representative (LAR) will authorize. In the case of an adult with a LAR, the LAR will authorize. The authorization provides consent to release otherwise confidential and protected personal information.
Health Insurance Portability and Accountability Act or HIPAA	Reflects how information is released, be it hard copy or digital. This form of release is secure but can take a long time. In some cases, it's been known to take well over a month. Only what's essential is released, not a generic copy of the full record.
Health Information Technology for Economic and Clinical Health or HITECH	Reflects how information is released. This format is secure but fast. Some circumstances cannot wait three days let alone 30 days. Only what's essential is released, not a generic copy of the full record. You may have noticed your specialists and PCP can view your electronic health record simultaneously and in real time. Consequently, these systems come with enhanced privacy and security features.

All that said, ROIs alone are not the only legal concern. Just because clients have rights to their files, we must thoroughly review every page before we give it to a client. How do we mitigate this concern? First, know your agency's protocol and follow it. When in doubt, speak with your supervisor or a designated proxy. Second, I casually inquire regarding the intended use of the record so I may better assist. Many documents aren't germane to many objectives. This can save the client money and agency personnel time. Third, is there something within those pages that may distress the client? For example, a client may have a "histrionic" response to something. The word "histrionic" is a legitimate clinical term, but it means some thing else in everyday parlance. I highlight the word and mark the page so I'll discuss it with the client. I do this for every page I'm dispensing. Fourth, when I contact the client that the documents are ready, I make an appointment to discuss content. I explain: *A clinical record sometimes uses language that has a clinical meaning that differs from how you may define it. The differences actually protect you from prying eyes. But that also means you might misinterpret it. I like to explain all such instances before I give you copies to avoid misunderstanding.* When the client arrives, we review each marked page together. In fact, I initial each highlighted segment to ensure I reviewed it.

Finally, there is final circumstance that may require input from an agency's legal counsel. An added benefit of the review I described above is that it can capture documents in the client record that are egregious and/or can potentially harm a client. The volume of notes entered into clinical records is vast, particularly in community mental health where thousands of clients receive services. Supervisors and quality assurance departments, despite their random audits, cannot reasonably monitor all the notes. I've known only two and went through the laborious process of purging one. The purged note was completely unrelated to the client's response to treatment. In fact, its author wanted to "vent" about a colleague and used the clinical note to do it. The other note was an email to a client that clearly reflected the professional's frustration with that challenging client. That email remained a part of the clinical record as did an addendum that captured the professional's in-person apology to the client and the client's response to it.

SUPERVISION: SUPERVISOR & SUPERVISEE COMPETENCE

How we manage chaos determines our trajectory

28

INTRODUCTION

This supervision section contains resources that can support practicing supervisors and supervisors of supervisors. While its primary audience is clinical supervisors, it is valuable as a crosswalk to clinical mental health counselors, child and family therapists, rehabilitation counselors, social workers, and others who supervise in the various disciplines covered by the umbrella term "helping profession".

You may ask yourself why this is included in a book about therapy basics. The fact is, MA level graduates are more likely to supervise than doctoral level graduate. And yet…

And yet, most MA level students don't receive the training doctoral level students receive on supervision. There are many reasons for this, the primary being that another course increases the already substantial MA graduation requirement. This guide is a first step to remedying that.

This guide is **NOT** a text that contextualizes the past, present, and future of supervision research, education, and practice of supervision. It's a tool to introduce you to the profession of supervision.
This guide is **NOT** a short-cut. Nothing can replace formal supervision training.

This guide is **NOT** a way to ensure your competence or save you more time than in-depth training that combines didactic and experiential elements. Think about why.

This guide is **NOT** a way to ensure your competence or save you more time than in-depth training that combines didactic and experiential elements. Think about why.

This guide is **NOT** about perpetuating myths. Being a competent clinician does not mean you'll be a competent supervisor. That's like saying a good piano tuner is a good pianist. Believing a myth doesn't make it a reality.

If you understand supervision, you will understand how to use it to become a stronger practitioner. It's not about control, although that happens. Supervision protects clients and you. It protects clients and you by ultimately helping you self-supervise: "*I always hear my supervisor in my head*." There it is.

Finally, and this might seem out of sequence, a few words on supervisory documentation. The time to document thoroughly is not when concerns develop. Memory being what it is, document supervision thoroughly from the start: date, time, situation, supervisee report, supervisor response, follow-up. This isn't in case problems arise. It's simply good, ethical and, to some degree, legal practice. Documentation, like the clinical note, reflects something that happened. Competent and responsible supervision is anchored in thorough documentation that captures supervisor as well as supervisee activities in an otherwise busy profession.

A Very, Very Brief History of Supervision

Most professionals attribute the origin of supervision to Freud's Wednesday Psychological Society meetings with his colleagues to present and consult on client cases. As psychotherapy increased in structure and accountability, the need for a professional intermediary between the service provider and client became increasingly clear. Supervisors, especially in today's multi-tiered healthcare system, were charged with teaching and monitoring service delivery to protect service recipients. Today, supervisors meet those obligations for students, associate licensees, and independent licensees. Observation and didactic methods are the primary tools for the exploration of the clinician's skills and limitations. If all this sounds tidy, it isn't. The debate, and the myths, continue to riddle one of the pillars of clinical practice. Not even laws and ethical standards can fully unzip myths into reality.

PERPETUAL SUPERVISION MYTHS

DOMAIN	MYTH	MYTH CORRECTED
Identity & Training	Having received supervision, we know how to provide it.	Supervision is a unique profession with legal and ethical responsibilities. Anyone who cannot have difficult discussions with supervisees need not apply. Skills required in supervision are not those used in therapy. The role requires specific training that directly impacts client recovery: Those who receive mediocre or poor supervision often don't professionally develop as they should and, consequently, may not deliver services appropriately. Thus, mimicking the supervision you received may not be the best way of ensuring competence.
Training Method	Can be acquired via reading or lecture	Like all higher degree professions, training involves demonstration, oversight, and feedback. Learning involves one side of the brain. Practice the other side.
Bad Supervisees	There are only good supervisors and bad supervisees	Many companies fail to meet their ethical and legal obligations to clients and supervisees, and waste vast amounts of money by not attending to high turnover rates.
Purpose	• Personal growth • Behavior changes • Self-understanding *No, that's therapy* • Ensure compliance with agency and regulatory body's policies and procedures • Clarify agency expectations, P & Ps, ensure compliance *No, those are admin supervision*	• Agency-dependent agenda • Improved client care • Improved service delivery • meets ethical and legal obligations
Essential Tasks	• Behavioral, cognitive, and affective process including listening, exploring, teaching *No, those are client-centered services*	• Teach/Ensure specific skills, evaluate performance against the standard, ID learning objectives
Timeframe	• Based on supervisee needs *No, that's client-centered timeframe*	• Weekly, Monthly, Continuous

DOMAIN	MYTH	MYTH CORRECTED
Outcome	• Open-ended, based on supervisee needs *No, that's client-centered outcome* • Consistent use of approved formats, policies, and procedures *No, that's admin supervision*	• Enhanced proficiency in knowledge, skills, and attitudes essential to effective job performance

29

ATTACHMENT & SUPERVISION

Attachment plays a factor in supervision because of countertransference. Attachment is characterized by behaviors within relationships, starting in early childhood between children and primary caregivers, caregivers who wield emotional and physical power. In adulthood, attachment styles describe attachment patterns in meaningful relationships. The supervisory relationship cannot be ignored in this respect.

Consistent care concludes in trust. Confidence is anchored in the primary supports in one's life. A bad supervisor can cause a lot of damage. **Early experiences are decisive**. That confidence is forged during early development - infancy, childhood, and adolescence – of professional development. **Expectations** can be linked to experiences, which can remain relatively fixed for a person's life. *Will my supervisor be there for me, even when I make dumb mistakes?* Who doesn't make dumb mistakes in the beginning? That's not different from: *I was bad yesterday. Will mama still love me?* Expectations. We expect from the future what we received in the past.

ATTACHMENT	DEFINED
----*Closeness trait*	Need to be near those we're attached to
----*Safe place trait*	When fearful or threatened, return to the primary attachment figure for comfort and safety
----*Are you my mom trait*	Primary attachment figures are the base of security from which children explore the surrounding environments
----*Separation anxiety trait*	Occurs in the absence of the primary attachment figure
Secure-in-the-storm attachment	Note: They accept comfort from others when the caregiver is absent, but they have a clear preference. Greater empathy in later childhood, well-behaved, more mature than children of other styles. Parents of these children play more with them and are more responsive to their needs. **As children, they:** -separate from caregivers -seek comfort from caregivers when frightened -Greet returning caregivers with happiness -Prefers parents to strangers **As adults, they have:** -Have trusting, lasting relationships, where feelings are shared -Have healthy self-concept -Seek social supports
So-So attachment (rare)	**As Children** -Cautious of strangers -highly distressed when parents leave -Uncomforted when parents return **As Adults** -Reluctant to be close to others, worry partners do not love them -distraught when relationships end
I-don't-think-so attachment	**As children** -May avoid caregivers -Do not seek much caregiver contact or comfort -little to no preference for caregivers over strangers **As adults** -possible intimacy problems -Invest little emotion in social and romantic relationships -Unwilling or unable to share thoughts or feelings with others

ATTACHMENT	DEFINED
Dysregulated attachment	**As toddlers** -show a mixture of avoidant and resistant behavior -may seem dazed, confused, or apprehensive **At 5 or 6** -may take on a parental role -some children may act as a caregiver toward the parent **As adults** -exhibit a confusing mix of anxious and avoidant behaviors - strong need for closeness, but struggle to be vulnerable. - may seek a loving relationship, but have difficulty trusting and push the person away - sabotage their relationships. -associated with unhealthy relationships – cling, poor communication, toxicity, and abuse.

ATTACHMENT IN SUPERVISION

SUPEE → SUP ↓	Secure	Anxious-Preoccupied	Dismiss-Avoid	Fear-Uncertainty
Secure	Both comfortable with seeking/ providing support	Supee fears autonomy, continuously seeks sup's approval	Supee, concerned re being perceived as incompetent, doesn't seek sup support	Supee unpredictable in pursuit of sup support as is perceptions of sup
Anxious-Preoccupied Sup	Sup anxious for supee autonomy, is overly directive. Supee feels restrained in professional growth	Sup, uncomfortable with supee autonomy, works with a supee who fears it. Supee is satisfied	Sup provides too much guidance for supee. Supee feels restrained in professional growth	Supee sees sup as supportive and controlling. When sup sets boundaries, supee retaliates

SUPEE → SUP ↓	Secure	Anxious-Preoccupied	Dismiss-Avoid	Fear-Uncertainty
Dismiss-Avoid Sup	Sup more comfortable with a supee's attempts for independence + need for supported. Supee confused by the lack of support or questions own competence.	Sup uncomfortable with supee "neediness" and avoidance of autonomy. As sup presses for supee autonomy, supee "need" increases	Both uncomfortable with seeking/providing support. Alliance appears to function, but supee unable to achieve necessary insight to succeed in role	Sup uncomfortable with supee affect and supee perceives sup as unpredictable. Alliance is tense, with sup providing minimal support needed to pacify an unpredictable supee
Fear-Uncertainty Sup	Sup wants, but fears, intimacy. Supee experiences sup as unpredictable. A securely attached supervisee may feel responsible for managing the affect in the relationship. This can lead to resentment or avoidance on the part of the supervisee.	Anxious supee initially responsive to unresolved sup for dependence needs. This alliance declines as supee realizes sup cannot manage supee's feelings	Supee, uncomfortable with managing sup's affect, avoids supervision	Unhealthy alliance: confused, hostile

30

CORE SUPERVISION PRINCIPLES

Competent supervision can mitigate risk and save money. It enhances the quality of direct and indirect client care; improves efficiency in service delivery; ensures professionalism; increases workforce satisfaction and retention; and upholds the ethical-legal agreement established long ago between the our disciplines and the public.

CORE PRINCIPLES

PRINCIPLE	DESCRIBED
Profession	Supervision is a demanding profession, not an escape hatch from direct service. The elephant in the room – transference. Some supervisors coerce their supervisees to engage in behaviors the supervisors could not. I've seen strong practitioner leave their roles and the profession as a result.
Competence	Competent practitioner ≠ competent supervisor. Far from it. Of course, they share some traits; but they mandate different essential skills.
EBPs	Clinical supervision ensures appropriate integration of and adherence to EBPs.

PRINCIPLE	DESCRIBED
Feedback skill	If as a supervisor you cannot provide feedback in a timely, balanced, and non-apologetic manner as needed without struggling, and don't want to seek help in learning, find another role. It's going to be a tense professional life knowing what you know you're not doing.
Crucible of client care I	Clinical supervision is a key component of clinical programs. It is the activity that marries mission and philosophy to clinical theory and evidence-based practices (EBPs) and safety. It exists only because, human nature being what it is, we often inaccurately report what we did.
Crucible of client care II	Supervision, therefore, exists to protect clients. In some cases, to protect them from practitioners and supervisors that may cause harm. A supervisor's priority is the client, not the supervisee. Sadly, thousands of practitioners seek and acquire their independent licenses and stop supervision, relieved that such an onerous process has ended. Of course, community mental health agencies that accept state and federal funds maintain the practice of supervision. In Arizona, once per month; which is reasonable. I've never understood how something so keenly linked to legal and ethical standards of client welfare holds so little of the profession's attention when we each know at least one licensed professional who shouldn't practice. I rest my case.
Direct or recorded observation of delivered services	Absolutely requires direct observation – live or recorded. Direct observation is the most effective method to measure counselor skills and client welfare, supervisee self-report the least. Training during direct observation is key to minimizing the negative and maximizing the positive effects of supervisee work. One method of observation is sitting in on the therapeutic session. Discuss this thoroughly with the supervisee and plan carefully. Some supervisee training concerns cannot be resolved *ad hoc*, but *in vivo*. A supervisee who doesn't take initiative and relies on being "nice" needs more than talk supervision. First, I restrict myself to a maximum of 3 interruptions during the sessions. Second, I cue the supervisee per an established subtle cue. Third, the supervisee turns to me seeking assistance. I model. When modeling doesn't work, I ask a confederate to act as a client without alerting the supervisee to that fact. The goal of "session" is to allow the supervisee to practice taking initiative instead of being "nice".

PRINCIPLE	DESCRIBED
Objective data or opinion?	Since supervision exists to protect the client, it will be anchored in objective data, not supervisee self-report or supervisor conjecture. It's important on both professional and legal fronts to know what typically transpires during sessions. There is also another reason - clients do not file formal complaints as often as I believe they could. They come to us when not "up to par", when more vulnerable. They are clients. All the ethic codes, all the cries for justice and parity mean nothing if this basic tenet is unmet. I regularly observe all supervisees assigned to me in their delivery of services. If you cannot respond with "yes", that's it. Any explanation is defensive. When things go sideways, supervisors are in the crosshairs. Research annual liability insurance pay-outs.
Ethical and legal: gatekeep	Model highest ethical, legal standards, and solutions to concerns as they emerge. Despite human fallibility, supervisors are tasked to model how to respond not only ethically, but also legally
Ethical and legal: Norms	-Ethical standards provide the what, not the how. They are purposely global for the continuous and active process that is ethics - Ethical decision making emerges from a tension between two positions. The most common one is confidentiality and when to breach it. Is it in the other person's best interest or not to speak to another individual or group to ensure wellness or safety? Sometimes, there is no clear "best" response. -One (1) hour supervision/week for non-independent licenses* -One (1) hour supervision/month for independent licenses* - Ensure client safety and quality care, which mandates monitoring staff written and behavioral performance. ---Educate staff re supervision and its legal-ethical requirements. ---Provide SMART formative and regular summative feedback for continuous individual professional development. * Depends on caseload size and composition (practitioners with large caseloads or who work with challenging clients - personality disorders, para/suicide among others – require more supervision. Monitor caseload size carefully.
Ethical and legal: Direct liability	Legal cases or case settlements will respond to the question: Did the supervisor respond reasonably or in dereliction of supervisory responsibility - negligence or omission of "reasonable" evidence to supervise. In short, the supervisor is liable for damages incurred for supervising improperly. Examples include inappropriate or no guidance regarding a client – mandated reporting or essential assessment. See * below

PRINCIPLE	DESCRIBED
Ethical and legal: Vicarious liability or *respondeat superior*	Responsibility for wrongful actions of **another** person: *Principal*: liable for wrongful acts of subordinates. *Parental*: parent/LAR liable for wrongful acts of person receiving guardianship. *Employer*: liable for wrongful act(s) of employee(s) See ** below
Ethical and legal: Confidentiality	Supervisors have a duty of care to clients, supervisees, students. Depending on professional setting, note 3 levels of informed consent: treatment, client consent to practitioner's supervision, and supervisee consent to supervision. With these comes a supervisor's implied consent and confidentiality as well as obligations to supervisory legal and ethical standards. Duty to report, duty to warn. standards determined by state legal and legislative systems. **Agencies tend to protect the agency and persons of greater authority – seek state licensure and legal counsel re codes of confidentiality and privileging.** ***Client and supervisees will understand these prior to services or supervision.***
Ethical and legal: Boundaries Most common ethical and legal complaint	Between practitioners and clients, between supervisees and supervisors. In some cases, relationships may pre-date the power-differential. In the case of client and practitioners, the solution is simple – practitioner recuses self. In the case of supervisee-supervisor, the supervisor will broach the topic with own supervisor and with the pending supervisee to seal potential concerns, paying close attention to unforeseen concerns. Focus: avoid harm, unequal power dilemmas - transference, counter-t.
Ethical and legal: Contract & Informed consent	Protective factors that ensure informed decisions, although who supervises often lacks "choice". Specifics re supervisory process, formative-summative feedback and evaluation and need for observation, role obligations and expectations. See sample. Depending on professional setting, note 3 levels of informed consent: treatment, client consent to practitioner's supervision, and supervisee consent to supervision. With these comes a supervisor's implied consent and confidentiality as well as obligations to supervisory legal and ethical standards.

PRINCIPLE	DESCRIBED
Ethical and legal: Technology	Websites and social media offer advise as if it's jelly beans. Online work requires specific training. Do not be fooled by it's apparent simplicity. -maintain confidentiality according to code and law -ensure practitioner competence and qualifications for online services. EX: States differ in child legal age to independently seek services -establish practice and reporting requirements, especially across state and national lines -self-report is highly unreliable -what you do not see on the computer screen can hurt you -see your governing/licensure body for resources
Ethical and legal practice II	Supervision is foundational to ethical-legal practice. It is where ethical-legal tenets are translated into action; where they are challenged, modelled, developed, and reinforced. a. Is there a potential for harm either personally, professionally, or clinically? In what way might this go beyond a personal issue to the agency or the profession? b. What are the relevant facts? Have all involved parties been contacted? What is unknown? Who has a stake in the outcome? c. What are obvious options for action? What would a reasonable person, counselor, or colleague do in a similar situation? What is the good-harm ratio for each action? d. What are alternative actions? What is the good-harm ratio for each action? What are the issues regarding justice, self-advocacy, non-malfeasance? e. How do you account for your own motives? Blind spots? If you can give the situation time, how would your motives change? f. Which is the best path of action? Before implementing it, consult with one or more knowledgeable others. Repeat as needed. g. Act on the path of action eventually selected. What were the outcomes? Knowing what you know now, would make the same selection? forced for ethical decision-making.

PRINCIPLE	DESCRIBED
Ethical and legal practice III	a. never ask a supervisee to do what they'd be unwilling to do. Why? Because supervisors carry the load, they do not to create them. b. demonstrate skills before they ask supervisees to engage in a new behavior. c. earn each supervisee's trust and respect. They inspire, coach, teach, encourage, motivate, communicate honestly and clearly, listens, believes there are multiple paths to most destinations, and demonstrate risk-taking. They inspire more than they command. d. have character, are mature, have vision, remained poised under pressure, and know how to lead. Leaders … ---Don't give orders to prove they're the boss. ---Take responsibility for decisions and give credit as due. ---Place supervisee growth before personal accomplishments. ---Take appropriate risks that are in the best interests of clients, supervisees, and the agency. ---Protect and advocate for supervisees, esp. with administrators. ---Buffer supervisees from rapid changes. ---Don't have favorites. e. manage ambivalence, hostility, and confrontation that can naturally arise in response to calls for change. f. know an exaggerated response (e.g., too defensive, too directive) can be as bad as no response. g. distinguish, and help supervisees distinguish, between counseling and supervision. "What does this have to do with counseling functions? How does this affect the supervisee's relationship with clients?"
Professional development	Supervision (a) ensures quality client care through continuous and systematic practitioner professional development; and (b) ensures the integrity of the counseling profession through the gatekeeping practice. Supervisors are required to maintain professional standards; attend to, recognize, and address supervisee and own impairment; and safeguard client welfare. These include counseling some individuals from the counseling profession. Wanting to be a therapist is not the same as being a competent therapist. The gatekeeping function is especially important during graduate student field placements as well as training development and credentialing.
Need never ends	Supervision meets the professional needs of practitioners regardless of skill and experience levels. Therefore, the frequency and format of supervision depends on each practitioner's knowledge base, stage of development, and client needs.

PRINCIPLE	DESCRIBED
Leadership	Supervision requires leadership that is knowledgeable, understands, and supports supervisors for an atmosphere that genuinely values and promotes professional development.
Knowledge base	Clinical practitioners have a knowledge base and field experience requisites. Supervision does not at the MA level.
Geo-socio-political shifts	Supervision influences and is influenced by these factors. Life, after all, is complicated. Supervisors will address the supervisee's response to clients, the supervisor's response to supervisees, and the program's response to its community.

Direct v. Vicarious Liability

Supervisors are legally responsible for each client on each supervisee's caseload. For agencies that assign more than seven supervisees per supervisor, that presents a dilemma that can be counterbalanced by a supervisor's self-advocacy and a personal liability policy. I recommend personal liability policies for practitioners, but especially supervisors regardless of the number of supervisees. When something goes wrong, agencies protect themselves first. This isn't a judgement on agencies. It's a reality. Protect yourself before you wish you had. The cost is minimal and you'll sleep better.

EX: If a supervisor oversees seven practitioners (peer supports, case managers, associate practitioners, independent practitioners) who each have 20 clients on their caseload, the supervisor is legally responsible for 140 clients and is expected to know each case.

EX: Not making a reasonable effort to supervise - negligent supervision. Negligent supervision includes not knowing what a supervisee is doing, failing to provide oversight, failing to teach, failing to keep supervision sessions, or failing to provide structured supervision.

One can easily see from the first example above how the supervisor's vulnerability increases as the number of supervisees increases and as each supervisee's caseloads increases. That said, when does a supervisor find time to directly observe, or review recorded sessions?

EX: providing inappropriate or incorrect advice to a supervisee about a client (disregard suicidal/homicidal screenings, report to child or adult protection agencies), failure to review supervisee caseload and listen attentively to what is said and unsaid, failure to assign cases based on training and availability of support for cases.

31

SUPERVISION METHODS

The supervision theory I use depends largely on the supervisee. What is the use of a psychoanalytically based supervision method with a supervisee who only wants concrete feedback? Some supervisees don't want to use supervision to discuss how they reached Y from X. They want to learn, to re-route their journey in as straight a line as possible.

So, be as familiar with supervision theories just as you are with clinical theories, to create the best "fit" between supervision and supervisee. Supervision isn't about you. It's about the supervisee, by proxy for clients.

THERA-PY-BASED	DEVELOPMENTAL	SOCIAL ROLE
Psychodynamic	Integrated Developmental	Discrimination
Person-Centered	*Eight-Task* - competence, emotional awareness, autonomy, identity, respect for differences, purpose/ direction, motivation, ethics. Three-Stage - stagnation, confusion, integration	*Systems Approach*: provides sups w/ map for strategic use of 7 factors that influence teaching and learning, where supervisory alliance is center. 3 phases of supervisory relationship: initial, mature, ending.

THERAPY-BASED	DEVELOPMENTAL	SOCIAL ROLE
Cognitive-Behavioral	*Six-Phase Supervision*: lay helper, beginning student, advanced student, novice professional, experienced professional, senior professional. Skovholt, Rønnestad	*Seven-Eyed* (clt, intervention, clt-clin relationship, clin process, clin-sup relationship, sup process, wider context foci). Relational focus on relationships b/w clt, clin, sup. Systemic focus on interplay b/w the three and the wider system. Important supees are aware of each eye, not memorize each.
Systemic		
Constructivist		
Narrative		
Solution-Focused		
Competence-based		Focus on supee skills, learning needs, SMART goals. 3 goals: (a) use social learning principles - model role reversal, role play, practice; (b) demonstrate; (c) teach, consult
Authoritative	No longer recognized as effective	No longer recognized as effective

SUPERVISION MODELS

Considerations:

1. Explicitly broach supervisee differences and factors associated with the differences.
2. Explicitly include supervisee concerns about specific client differences from the supervisee, address the factors associated with the differences.
3. Explicitly broach supervisee concerns about services in multiracial communities and the essential networking needed.

While it is key to articulate a philosophy of change, identify a core model of practice and supervision, keeping in mind that supee needs and skills drive the final selection. For example, I prefer DBT for most of my clinical practice but a client with moderate to high developmental disabilities is unlikely to benefit from DBT without serious modifications. The same applies to supervision – it will "fit" the supervisee if it is to help the client. Theories frame knowledge and facilitate knowledge transfer. It is when we make sense of knowledge that we're able to transfer it into action in as salient a way as possible for the supervisee and, ultimately, the client. All this said, it's imperative not to confuse service delivery with supervision. Complete the points below to focus your supervisory model selection:

1. Beliefs about how people change in treatment and supervision

2. Factors key to treatment and supervision

3. Universal principles to treatment and supervision

4. What does good supervision include?

32

SUPERVISOR & SUPERVISEE DEVELOPMENTAL LEVELS

Supervisor Developmental Levels

Developmental models frame and explain why a new supervisor behaves differently from a seasoned one. Note that supervisors typically reside at the second or third level of counselor development.

LEVEL	SUP TRAIT	SKILLS NEEDED
1	• anxious • naïve about supervisor role • focused on the "right" thing • overresponds as an "expert" • uncomfortable providing clear and direct feedback	• Follow structure and formats • implement systems to organize supervision • work with Level I supervisees
2	• confused and conflicted • supervision is complex and multidimensional • needs support to maintain motivation • Overfocused on supervisee limitations/ deficits and "resistance" • unconsciously becomes a therapist with supervisee	• Provide supervision of supervision • work with Level 1 supervisees

3	• anchored in method • highly motivated • provides honest self-appraisal of own supervisory strengths and weaknesses • comfortable with evaluation processes • provides ethical and legal, objective and outcome oriented, honest, compared to a standard, balanced, clear, immediate, non-apologetic, consistent, supportive, increases supervisee mastery	• work with any supervisee level

Supervisee Developmental Levels

Regardless of the supervision model applied, development cannot be ignored - level of training, experience, proficiency. Different supervisory approaches fit supervisees at different stages of development.

1. There is a beginning, but no end to learning skills; be careful of "know it alls".
2. Account for individual personalities and learning styles. Fit the supervisory approach to the supervisee's developmental stage.
3. Development occurs chronologically, logically, and flexibly. Some can practice for years and still remain at an early developmental level while another can progress through the levels quickly.
4. Different tasks can have different levels. A supervisee can be excellent at case management and limited in group work.

LEVEL	SUPEE TRAIT	SUP SKILL NEEDED
1	• focus on self • anxious, uncertain • preoccupied with the right way • Overconfident of skills • Overgeneralizes • Overuses a skill • Gap between conceptualization, goals, and interventions • Ethics underdeveloped	• structure to minimize anxiety • Support, address strengths first, then weaknesses • Suggest approaches • connect theory to treatment Technique: • observation • skills training • role play • readings • group supervision • closely monitor clients
2	• Focus less on self, more on client • confused, frustrated with work complexity • overidentifies with client • challenges authority • no integration with theoretical base • overwhelmed • ethics better understood	• less structure, more autonomy • Supportive • periodic suggestion of approaches • speak to discrepancies • introduce alternative views • process comments, transference/ countertransference, affective reactions to client and/ or supervisor Technique: • observation • role play • Interpret dynamics • group supervision • reading
3	• Focus on client • highly empathic • Objective perspective • integrative in thought and approach • very responsible and ethical	• supervisee directed • focus on personal-professional integration and career • supportive • change agent Technique • peer supervision • group supervision • reading

Key Principles

There's no denying that supervision is expensive, regardless of the setting. It, nevertheless, more than pays for itself, assuming the organization has competent supervisors. Supervision results in satisfied and ethical practitioners who uphold the law and professional standards, quality services, and organizational efficiency. That proves the importance of key principles in supervision.

PRINCIPLE	DESCRIBED
Requires administration support	Practitioners need a milieu conducive to timely and professional growth. They do the heavy lifting.
Typically balances clinical and administrative needs	The two needs can complement and conflict, creating a real tension for supervisors. With training, not the assumption that a good practitioner makes a good supervisor, the roles can be clarified and made more straightforward.
Necessity	It organizes and integrates missions, visions, goals, and philosophies, and integrity of evidence-based practices (EBPs). It systematically ensures quality services, client safety, and staff professional development. It is integral to morale and retention
Alliance	Supervision is all about the relationship. As in counseling, developing the alliance between the counselor and the supervisor is the key to good supervision.
Self-awareness & humility	Be human and have a sense of humor. As role models, you need to show that everyone makes mistakes and can admit to and learn from these mistakes.
A profession with unique skills to learn, practice, and develop	Good counselors do not make good supervisors. That is a myth that has cost organizations millions. Good supervisors, as members of an ethically and legally-based profession, require training and oversight to provide competent supervision. Supervisors will shift their orientation within a program and toward supervisees and clients to understand, internalize, and execute the new set of skills. Competent supervisors are molded, not discovered pre-existing. Know and practice therapeutic and supervision models for a sense of purpose. Before supervisors teach knowledge and skills, they will understand the foundation that undergirds supervision.
Regardless of expertise, every practitioner **and supervisor** needs supervision	Supervision is tailored to the practitioner's knowledge base, skills, experience, and assignment. Frequency and intensity of supervision and training depend on the role, skill level, and client population. Supervision benefits even the seasoned practitioner since self-awareness is never 100%.
Where competent and ethical practitioners develop and mature.	Supervisors guide and model ethical and legal practice. In this way, supervisees learn to self-supervise. In supervision, questions are discussed before they become problems, ethical practice is bridged from construct to behavior that can be generalized to various circumstances.

PRINCIPLE	DESCRIBED
Where supervisors meet their mandatory ethical and legal gatekeeping obligation	Supervisors model and maintain professional and ethical standards. They address practitioner impairment via observation, record review, performance evaluations – formative and summative feedback – and recommendations to credentialing bodies to protect clients. That task alone means they are subject to legal liability. Some practitioners and students can be helped, fewer will be counseled from the profession - gatekeeping function.
Clinical supervision will include direct observation. Without this, only a partial picture of supervisee competency is visible	Direct observation is the catalyst for competence and *the* method for building skills and quality services. Accomplishing those tasks requires training in objective observation, provision of clear and balanced feedback, and the development of growth plan. Any supervision session without observation is guesswork. Self-reports tend to be self-serving, not out of maliciousness, but from instinct.
Contextual variables that include interpersonal differences	To be respectful is to identify and/or broach differences between even seemingly similar individuals. If individuals in families differ markedly, ... How any one person responds to another or how an organization responds to clients determines the level of inherent respect. Supervisors are change agents, which requires them to understand others more than any other practitioner if supervisees are to address the plethora of needs that exist today. **Developmental phases in this domain:** ***The Gavel*** Dominant person or culture is right. This leads to problems, not the least of which is discrimination. ***Incapable*** Separate but equal treatment. Still leads to problems because still discriminates against the other ***Blind*** Sees everyone as equal. Can be true for very few. When partially true, it still discriminates through blinders ***Open*** Appreciates differences, especially those markedly different from self. That openness allows the person to work with a greater To be competent or proficient at this, know that each person has lived a separate existence from ourselves, even if it's a sibling.

PRINCIPLE	DESCRIBED
Essential to EBP implementation of and fidelity	Supervisors are key to EBP use. Current research suggests that it takes 10-15 years before an EBP is implemented accurately. During that time span, new EBPs sit on the shelf. It's startling. Supervisors, more than anyone else, are obliged to acquire and transfer knowledge, oversee it in their supervisees, and ensure no other EBPs are neglected. That is fidelity.
Model intra- and interpersonal boundaries	Ensure supervisees see you establish clear boundaries regarding professionalism, proper diet, and time off. Like it or not, others notice.

New Supervisors

HINT	EXAMPLES
Quickly learn … organizational P&Ps HR P&Ps	a. hiring and firing b. affirmative action c. accommodation d. limits to privacy e. feedback and evaluations
Quickly learn to speak HR	If you don't, you'll struggle to meet your needs.
Take 3-4 months to study supervision	a. Don't make any changes b. Listen, learn, ask questions, seek training c. seek supervision and guidance, peer/mentor support d. find your style and voice e. solicit feedback.
Learn about your supervisees	a. Review their files b. Schedule meetings to review the supervision contract and informed consent c. Discuss concerns, conflicts, goals, strengths, limitations, planned time away
Shadow a supervisor	Either within same location, another, or another organization if there's someone trusted there

HINT	EXAMPLES
Supervisee resistance to supervision	a. Internal promotion b. More experience in the profession c. Too little experience to understand the need for supervision d. differences: higher SES bracket, older, much younger, gender, race/ethnicity
Supervisee resistance: Hints	-What are possible origins of defensiveness? Address the root causes. -Accept, don't resist, resistance. Resistance is a natural response to the unknown, not a character flaw. Acknowledge and reasonably sympathize with their concerns. Pace yourself. -Create a positive alliance with staff. -Self-disclose experiences as a supervisee. It can help with anxious staff. -Be clear and consistent about communicating goals and expectations. -Always provide a sample of the standard so staff can compare their work against it. Will seem less supervisor-centered.

Informed Consent and Supervision Contract

Informed Consent

The written informed consent provides supervision dyad members protective factors from practical and legal concerns. It testifies that the supervisee is aware of the supervision intervention, its objective of client protection, potential risks and alternative approaches, and can make an informed and intelligent decision about participating in that intervention. It also testifies the supervisor clearly articulated, verbally and in writing, the supervision process, feedback and evaluation criteria, other supervisory tasks and documents, and the remediation process among other processes. The signed supervision informed consent, in tandem with the signed supervision contract, testify that the dyad understands and agrees with the process of supervision.

You may be thinking: Do we have control over who supervises us? Fair point. In many settings, the supervisee-supervisor matching process is perfunctory not strategic. In reality, supervisees are assigned to the available supervisor unless it is a case of re-assignment. In such cases, the agency locates a substitute supervisor. This is not always easy to achieve, particularly in rural communities.

True, technology can facilitate the process, but there are limits to the number of supervision hours offered remotely. The material differences between in-person and remote interactions are not yet breached.

INFORMED CONSENT DOMAIN	VARIABLES
Ethics, Law	• Conduct • Supervisees number • Emergency and back-up supervisors • Consults for ethical dilemmas • Confidentiality limits in supervision • Confidentiality limits in triadic, group, and peer supervision • Boundaries and dual relationships • Supervisee boundaries: self-care, burnout, transference, countertransference •
Purpose	• Theoretical models • SMART Goals of supervision • Goals, formative and summative evaluations, timeframes • Clear supervisee and supervisor role definitions and expectations •
Professional Disclosures	• Theoretical orientation • Supervisor educational background & credentials • Supervisor training • Competence • Training and professional goals •
Process/Format	• Individual, triadic, group, peer • Direct observation how to • Remediation • Ensure supervisee informed client re parameters of counseling and supervision (esp. live or recorded observation) •
Due Process	• Complaints and grievances • Written procedure •
Statement of Agreement	• Everyone's signature •

Written Supervision Contract

The written supervision contract protects the rights of the agency, the supervisor, and supervisee. It is a contractual agreement supervisor and supervisee that states the purpose, goals, and objectives of supervision. The written supervision contract, in tandem with the signed supervision consent, testifies to the supervisee's awareness and agreement with supervision.

SUPERVISION CONTRACT DOMAIN	VARIABLES
Minimum Duties and Responsibilities	***Supervisee …*** • Uphold ethical guidelines, legal statutes • Be prepared to discuss all client cases • Discuss approaches and techniques used • Timely consult about emergencies, and boundary or ethical concerns • Implement and document supervisor directives • Adhere to agency policies and procedures • ***Supervisor …*** • Uphold ethical guidelines, legal statutes • Intervene immediately and clearly if client welfare is at risk • Review all psychosocial histories, progress notes, treatment plans, and discharge plans • Supervisee justifies selected approach and techniques • Present, model, and observe clinical interventions • Monitor supervisee community collaboration and networking • Adhere to agency policies, procedures •
Purpose, SMART Goals, SMART Objectives	--Purpose: client welfare, gatekeep the profession --Goals, objectives: ----Promote supervisee development and disposition: positive interpersonal skills, work ethic, accountability, professional development ---Promote service competence: assessment, service planning, documentation, treatment modality, when and when not to apply theoretical frameworks ----Monitor supervisee performance ----Increase supervisee's self-supervision for increased independence ----Balance 4 essential functions: administrative, evaluative, supportive, clinical.
Provision	• Date, time, frequency of individual, triadic, group, and/or peer supervision according to client contact hours • Supervision model and case review format • Clients gave aware of and need for supervisee supervision • Client progress reviewed per acuity and on a rotating basis •
Context	--Non-independently licensed supervisee: One hour weekly and as indicated --Independently licensed supervisee: One hour monthly and as indicated

SUPERVISION CONTRACT DOMAIN	VARIABLES
Documentation	• Specify each form, it's purpose, and the use of its content • Use of supervision notes is at the supervisor's discretion, but always sensitive to supervisee's confidentiality • Formative feedback provided each session • Frequency of summative feedback and how it interfaces with formative feedback •
Evaluative Methods	--Formative: continuous across the learning process resulting in real-time adjustments. The focus is on the process leading to summative outcomes. Supervisee openness to feedback is key. Supervisor ability to communicate feedback in a manner the supervisee can manage is key. --Summative: occurs at the end of a specified period that determines if objectives were met. An example is the annual performance review or a review of student work at end of class that determines the grade, unlike the formative feedback. This evaluation is outcome-oriented, assessing the final product. Supervisee openness to feedback is key. Supervisor ability to communicate feedback in a manner the supervisee can manage is key.
Procedural Consideration	The Individual Development Plan's goals and objectives will be discussed and amended if necessary. • The quality of the supervisory relationship will be discussed and conflicts resolved. • If conflicts cannot be resolved, (name) will be consulted. • In the event of an emergency, the counselor is to contact the supervisor. If unavailable, contact (alternate's name, title, and other relevant back-up information). • Crises or emergency consultations will be documented. • Due process procedures (as explained in the agency's policy and procedure handbook) have been reviewed and will be discussed as needed
Supervisee Scope of Competence	Competencies related to students versus personnel
Supervisee duties and responsibilities	--Understand need for and elements of supervision --SMART Learning Goals and Objectives ----Documentation ----Practice ----Theory, methods
Supervisor's Scope of Competence	• Title/date of credentials/licensure. • Formal supervisory training and credentials. • Years providing supervision. • Current supervisory responsibilities

SUPERVISION CONTRACT DOMAIN	VARIABLES
Supervisor duties and responsibilities	--Primary obligation is to clients, secondary to supervisees --Provide data-based and observation-based feedback --Ensure necessary supervisee changes are attainable as documented – break down into manageable portions
Agreement	--Contract subject to change as initiated by supervisee and/or supervisor, but with consent of both. --At minimum, formal contract reviews occur annually or mid-term and end of term for students. --Supervisee and supervisor title, signature, date
General Considerations	IDs supervisee, supervisor, agency name with mobile numbers
	IF supervisee is a student, IDs student's university, program name, practicum or internship, semester.
	IDs back-up supervisor & mobile number
	ID got-to in case of conflict between supervisee and supervisor
	Each supervision session includes: --SMART supervisee goals and objectives: Review/Modify as necessary. --Data-based and balanced feedback: On clinical documentation, direct practice (recording, in-person, blind in-person), and other clinically related documents and practices (e.g., service plan, referrals) --Caseload progress: Review, highest acuity has priority. Typically, all clients addressed within 4 supervision sessions.

CLINICAL SUPERVISION METHODS

Method	Description	Advantage	Disadvantage
Self-Report	• Reports of clinical situations • Group discussion of clinical situations •	• Spontaneous and/or informal • Time efficient • Offers insight into supervisee case organization, what is included or eliminated from report, level of awareness and perspective, learning trajectory • Allows for contrast between supervisee report and sup observation	• Personal perspective can be inaccurate • Based on supervisee's sense of priority • Can become broad or philosophical instead of directly tied to identified client needs, EBPs, service plan •

Method	Description	Advantage	Disadvantage
Client Record Review	• Review of documentation (e.g., progress notes, service plan and updates) •	• Ensures supervisee competence • Ensures compliance with standards • A method of quality management • Ensures timeliness and consistency of record •	• Time consuming, most agencies have a QA department •
Case Consultation	• Review and discussion of client cases •	• Integrates theory and technique • Promotes self-awareness • Links client needs with service plan and provision • Organizes client data, needs, service gaps • Examines issues (e.g., cross-cultural issues) •	• Conceptualization accuracy can depend on supervisee developmental level and requires supervisory insight • Reflects specific skills not range of skills •
Direct Observation	• In-person observation of therapeutic •	• Teaches and ensures quality of care • Counselor can see and experience positive change in session direction in the moment • Allows sup to intervene when needed to protect the welfare of the client, if the session is not effective or is destructive to the client	• Intrusive • May result in client and supervisee anxiety • Time consuming • Sup comments will be limited •
Webcam Observation	• Internet supervision, synchronistic and asynchronistic • Teleconferencing •	• Versatile, efficient, inexpensive • Minimizes geographical distances • Can be stored and watched anywhere • Facilitates reflective practice (learn then apply to future work)	• Confidentiality concerns • May increase client or counselor anxiety or self-consciousness (tends to dissipate) • Technical training needed • Subject to technology malfunction • Will be protected from unauthorized individuals • Subject to subpoena if not destroyed •

Method	Description	Advantage	Disadvantage
Recorded Observation	• Audio or audio-visual recording of a counseling session •	• Non-intrusive, efficient, and inexpensive • Allows supervisee and sup to review in advance of supervision session • Explores a plethora of skills (e.g., relationship, non/verbal behavior, content, pacing, rapport, pace, interventions use) • provides concrete work examples • Provides a platform for alternate approaches • Can be used in group supervision • Augments summative feedback • Can be stored • Facilitates reflective practice (learn then apply to future work)	• Counselor may feel anxious (dissipates) • Subject to technology malfunction • Will be protected from unauthorized individuals • Subject to subpoena if not destroyed • Requires technology training •
Cofacilitation and Modeling	• Supervisee share a counseling session • Sup demonstrates a specific technique while the counselor observes •	• Allows the sup to model techniques • Gives supervisee "permission" to try risky techniques • Can be useful to the client ("two counselors for the price of one") • Sup will demonstrate proficiency in the skill and help the counselor incrementally integrate the learning • Supervisee sees, learns, applies sup response • Sup incrementally shapes the counselor's skill acquisition and monitors skill mastery • Allows sup to aid counselor with difficult clients •	• Requires additional session time • To be of greatest benefit, sup will be proficient, non-intrusive, and breaks down complicated techniques to help supervisee learn • May impact supervisee credibility with client •
Role Play	• Role play a clinical situation or use a skill demonstrated by the sup during co-facilitation •	• Fun • Supervisee sees, learns, applies sup response • Provides opportunity for shaping behavior • Increases supervisee comfort • Is safe for new or difficult skills •	• Supervisee anxiety • Sup will "chunk" new skill • May not translate into therapeutic work •

KEY ISSUES AND ACTIONS FOR ETHICAL CLINICAL SUPERVISORS

Issue	Action
Direct and vicarious liability	Address supervisory power of control; time, place, and purpose of each delivered service; rationale for supervisee clinical decisions and actions; supervisor's expectations for action.
	Supervisor makes a reasonable effort to supervise. Supervisor provides appropriate guidance. Avoids dereliction of duty. Ensures treatment does not result in harm, wrongdoing, or damage to the client, organization, or community. Assigns clinical tasks according to supervisee scope of competence and/or adjusts supervision accordingly.
Confidentiality	Adhere to laws of confidentiality (HIPAA, CFR) Balance of client and supervisee right to privacy and feedback/evaluation Adhere to duty to warn, report, and protect
Informed Consent and due Process	Clients and supervisees are fully informed about the approach, procedures, parameters, requirements of treatment and supervision. Required forms and documents are read and signed by all. A just process encourages conflict resolution and ensures the client's and supervisee's right to appeals.
Supervisor and counselor scope of competence	Supervisor and supervisee operate within their scope of practice and competence. Each meets minimal standards of competence regarding cultural and contextual awareness, knowledge, and skills. Each works effectively within a wider system of community services and institutions
Dual relationships	Differentiate between teaching and supervisory roles of students. Avoid (or reduce impact, if unavoidable) supervision of current or former clients, current or former romantic or sexual partners, business associates, family members, or friends. Avoid social activities with supervisees that may impair objectivity. Avoid excessive self-disclosure and comments or actions that might be interpreted as sexual. Respect professional boundaries in all aspects of professional relationships. Consult with experienced others and colleagues when in doubt.

Issue	Action
Diversity and cultural competence	Supervisors… ensure own, supervisee, and support staff continuous cultural competence via education and training, supervised clinical work.
	… explore and challenge own and each other's biases, assumptions, values, and worldviews (race, ethnicity, gender, religion, socioeconomic status, sexual orientation, ability) and relate them to attitudes, values, behaviors, and therapeutic and supervision processes.
	… explore helping approaches other than those based in American and northern European scholarship.
Unintentional disrespect	Well-intentioned supervisors can still be unaware of how differences – background, life experience, race, to name a few -- affects relationships with supervisees and, therefore, may not broach those variables. This includes differences between members of the same group.
Power dynamics	Differentials in power can be magnified, particularly in dyads, where the supervisor is a member of a dominant group and the supervisee is a member of a minority group
Trust and vulnerability	Supervisees are inherently in a vulnerable position and are expected to trust their supervisors, when they may or may not have reason to do so.
Communication	Since communication reflects culture, communication style can result in misunderstandings.

33

MORE ETHICS & GATEKEEPING

Supervisors have two primary functions. We safeguard client welfare through supervisee training and oversight. We also safeguard clients and the profession through our gatekeeping function. Client welfare is straightforward. Even if you don't think about it, the two words are the perfect book-ends. Strong, clear, solid. If that's not enough, look round. Client welfare has material and figurative eyes everywhere. Supervisees look to supervisors for guidance, the agency looks to them to keep client sentinel events at zero, and the law mandates them to know as much as possible about client progress to guard against what they may not know. Then, there's the paperwork. We're drowning in paperwork intended to safeguard clients. That's not an editorial comment; rather, it's the professional hammer that drives my nail home. Yes, there are a very few among us who are flippant, unaware, or too jaded to care; but the majority "believe' because, deep down, this work lends meaning to a life lived usefully.

Gatekeeping is another matter. Compared to client welfare... Look at it: gate, keeping. Could anything be more benign? At the risk of sounding flippant, gate and keeping or gatekeeping conjures images of an unsophisticated fence, against which someone rests, legs raised on one of its poles, straw hanging from lips. It's like a worn jacket - familiar. We genuflect at the continuing education altar, share the thresholds of our intestinal fortitude inside training break-out groups, collect the continuing education certificate, and there! another license renewal obligation met. We exit so fast that we fail to see we've left the gate unlatched.

We fail, I'm afraid, to deliberately plan for the solitary experience that is gatekeeping. But I'm getting ahead of myself. Here is the story in broad strokes. If you've supervised for at least one week and if you've practiced for at least one month, you'll recognize David.

Before I accepted the director role at Clinic X, I supervised a counselor seeking his independent license, the LPC. David was bright, motivated, and eager to leave his mark. Outside the supervision hour log that described each supervision session in three to five words, I received little to no documentation from the previous supervisor. I began supervision with the informed consent process, the supervision contract, defined supervisee and supervisor roles and responsibilities, collaborated on supervisee goals, and so on.

Within one week, I began to field concerns about David from his clients and peers. In general, the complaints were concerned with defensiveness, argumentativeness, more self-disclosure than necessary, the belief his approach was the "right" approach, and "telling me how high to jump" said one client. I immediately scheduled a meeting with David's previous supervisor. Her experiences mirrored mine.

I did my job. I documented each client and peer complaint and contacted each to understand the concerns. Peers, without exception, were unwilling to provide David with feedback. The majority of clients was willing to continue services with David; some were comfortable speaking to him alone, but a few requested my presence. In each case, before David met with a client, he and I discussed the client's concerns. We also reviewed the process of receiving feedback, specifically that while feedback needn't "fit", it will be heard respectfully without resorting to explanations. Finally, we identified a "signal" that meant I'd like to step outside briefly (we told clients we were getting drinks). I used the signal on two occasions to encourage him to listen to the client's feedback.

Those and other experiences became a part of twice weekly dyadic supervision that included observation (i.e., me, a peer from a sister clinic to ensure objectivity), SMART goals, and a performance enhancement plan.

Soon thereafter, I accepted the director role. David and I reviewed his progress, and discussed his transition to another supervisor. I also met with the new supervisor to debrief her on key points and transfer his supervision file. In less than one month, I resumed David's supervision. I hope you'll trust me about this -- Had I assigned him to the remaining supervisor, the outcome would have been the same, if not worse.

Fast forward… One morning, I opened a manilla envelope as I walked to my office. Time stretched as I saw it was David's board application for the LPC. I shut the door to my office, sat with the licensure endorsement form in front of me. There it was, the isolation of gatekeeping. That initial sensation of helplessness and vulnerability set it well apart from other supervisory activities.

I'll consult with my supervisor and he will agree with me. I'll consult with HR and they'll give me the legal nod. Peers will support me. A stranger on the street will support me, but that's not the point. That endorsement request was in *my* box.

Documentation in hand, I consulted with my supervisor and he agreed with me. HR gave me the legal nod.

I photocopied the supervision documentation and sealed it in an envelope; photocopied the endorsement page, completed it, wrote DRAFT across it; and knocked on David's door.

To say that meeting was unpleasant is an understatement. But as I shut David's office door as I left, I was struck by the symbolism of what I had done. If I close my eyes, I'm back there. There was something transcendent about concluding a task that's both unpleasant and compulsory. It's a reverse rite of passage. I felt innocent again, like a child. The experience peeled away that veneer we accumulate over time – I felt the mystery of what happens when one life intersects with another, all triviality removed. It was pure; and I'm now grateful my ego didn't get a craving to make it more than it was.

Fast forward four years... My home phone rings. A state licensure board investigator wants to interview me about David. *I'm happy to assist, but I severed David's relationship with the clinic four years ago. How could my input carry weight? Why should it?* The investigator explained that the Board compiled the data from all the interviews to weigh David's appropriateness as a counselor. *We take this as seriously as you do. The interviews, taken together, point to a trend of behavior.*

I passed that test.

ELEMENTS OF SMART FEEDBACK

ELEMENT	POOR EXAMPLE	GOOD EXAMPLE
Specific, measurable, achievable (developmentally based), realistic, timely (as close to observation or data gathering as possible)	You did a good job.	You made a good point regarding . . . I observed a specific and recurring behavior... Keep doing more of . . .
Formative FB: provided continuously during the learning process. Intended to improve work.	Didn't we talk about that already?	When you combine the FB about note length with the FB about clinical vocabulary: Your notes become briefer but comprehensive.

ELEMENT	POOR EXAMPLE	GOOD EXAMPLE
Summative FB: provided at discrete points after the learning process. Intended to facilitate global understanding of what was learned and how it impacts progress	This covers all the points we've been discussing the past few months.	Let's review your overall progress the past six months. We'll start with documentation
Statement, not question	What do you think of the length of your documentation?	Your notes are very detailed and, consequently, you're falling behind in your documentation.
Formative + Summative FB and the Informed Consent process	Neither FB reviewed and differentiated during the Informed Consent process	Formative and summative FB reviewed and differentiated during the Informed Consent process. Parameters to both clearly described as well as how formative informs summative.
Balanced (positive + constructive)	I've written all the FB out for you so you don't need to take notes. Please make the changes	Although your documentation is long, you have a talent for case conceptualization. You've reached the point where you can maximize one by minimizing the other.
Limit to 3 constructive statements	I've written them so we can quickly review all 7.	If we focus on these two items, I think we can address some of those needs you expressed earlier. Let's begin.
Direct, non-apologetic, unbiased, non-threatening, non-demeaning	I don't know how to say this, but what were you thinking?	You seemed to struggle with reflection of feeling in this session. Let's look at this together.
"What" not "why" orientation (observable, changeable behaviors)	Why did you do that?	I notice you're submitting documentation later each week.
Focus: supervisee development, specifically self-assessment	I think everything feels important to you and you use all your time trying to capture it all. The result: no time to write all your notes.	I notice you're completing documentation later each week. I imagine that's stressful. Let's take a look. I like watching you supervise yourself. What are your guesses as to barriers?

ELEMENT	POOR EXAMPLE	GOOD EXAMPLE
Anchored in supervisee professional goals and competencies	Everyone needs to learn how to develop a SMART ISP. I'll keep giving you FB.	When the client and you broke down her ISP objectives into manageable pieces, she became more motivated and began to achieve her goals. When you "knit" her progress/limitation to progress with those objectives into your notes, your notes became easier to write. You've achieved 2 goals: ISP development and ISP-driven documentation.
Data-based (recording, work samples) + the standard Not per supervisee self-report or supervisor opinion	I think you mentioned something about that last week – not being able to steer the session.	You found that section of the session recording where you have trouble steering away from "the how-do-you-dos". You go first. I like to hear you think.
Ensure supervisee understands FB prior to improvement suggestions by having supervisee repeat what was heard	This is simple. The first thing you do is…	I'd like to hear your thoughts about this FB. What fits, what doesn't fit for you?
Two-way process (even when objective, supervisor "owns" it; supervisor genuinely solicits FB that can inform supervisory practice)	You don't seem to understand…	We've identified how X can work better for managing Y. Now the final piece -- I can use your FB and suggestions. To be an effective supervisor means I need your FB.

It's important to note that consistent and objective formative feedback means summative feedback holds no surprises. That is especially true when the supervisee internalizes the formative feedback, resulting in behavioral change.

All Paths Lead to Competence

Anytime two people come together, you can be sure of one of two outcomes. One is an exchange of information that presumably leads to increased knowledge and intimacy – personal or professional. The other is nothing. Really. Even if the conversation was pleasant. This is what typically happens when two individuals, one a supervisee, the other a supervisor, meet. Absolutely nothing. Tiresome for the supervisee, and a lost opportunity for the supervisor. If only to safeguard clients, never mind promote the profession.

A supervisee who may enter supervision with child and marital problems feels overwhelmed by the stress of private life and the complex demands of professional one. Consequently, the supervisee may miss work and may often cancel client appointments when at work. The supervisor, for a variety of ethical and legal reasons, may simultaneously address the supervisee's job performance, provide professional emotional support, and avoid issues related to the supervisee's personal life. There are consequences.

CONSIDERATIONS:

1. The tension between private and professional stressors, awareness of how individuals vary in their demonstration of each.
2. Illuminate boundaries between clinical supervision and personal counseling, how to assist when personal counseling is needed
3. Monitor, document, and maintain adequate clinical performance when personal problems impact work performance.

Noor worked at a community mental health agency for two years. Among her many strengths, Noor is trilingual and, as a Christian from Beirut, understands the stresses and cultural dynamics faced by minority immigrants living in America. In Beirut, Noor trained and worked as a psychiatrist. She planned to complete a residency in psychiatry and sit for the state board after her husband completed both in internal medicine. Meanwhile, Noor applied her expertise to counseling and has been praised within the community for her efforts on behalf of refugees. Her seven-year-old son, diagnosed with Down's Syndrome at birth, attended elementary school on a part-time basis.

Due to her years of professional experience as a psychiatrist, Noor was assigned complex and difficult cases, and more of them than other practitioner. Her understanding of multiple diagnoses, and skill in therapeutic modalities and assessment made her a resource for many agency practitioners. Additionally, her caseload has grown even more due to a sudden increase in client census.

Noor was friendly and outgoing. Although she rarely discussed her private life, she hinted at a problem related to her husband and son during the last supervision session. Her supervisor, Kim, had observed a steady decline in energy and mood, and increased isolation. Kim also observed that while Noor met her professional obligations inside and outside supervision, she did so with less enthusiasm. Moreover, she arrived late to a few appointments in the past month and had started to reschedule appointments. Consequently, the first clients of each workday began to express their concerns to the front desk, who passed the information to Noor and Kim. During the past four weeks, Noor called in sick at least once each week.

During supervision, Noor was distracted and her case reports lacked their typical comprehensiveness. During the last supervision session, Kim asked how everything was and Noor grew tearful. Noor did not speak and Kim waited supportively. Noor broke the silence with "*I don't know what to do. My husband... My son... Can we talk another time?*" Kim was unsure whether Noor's question was an attempt to avoid further discussion or a need to seek her emotional support. She liked Noor and had they been peers, would have offered her assistance. But they were not peers, and Kim was uncomfortable with the idea of becoming Noor's confidant. Kim responded that they could return to it during the next supervisory session. They continued with the scheduled supervision session.

Between both sessions, Kim resolved to (a) clarify the difference between her ability to provide work-based and personal support and (b) discuss Noor's performance. She collected data on late arrivals to work, client expressions of concern, rescheduled appointments, and unscheduled time away.

Kim: *Noor, come in. Are you comfortable? Good. Before we start today, I'd like to discuss our last supervision session and explore how we can move forward together.*

Noor: *I'd like that, although I want to apologize. Work isn't the place for personal problems; and not for you to fix. When you were nice and asked if I was okay, it opened the spigot. I don't know. I'm embarrassed.*

Kim: *Noor, an apology isn't necessary, although I understand. Whatever it is, it's stressful enough to make you do things you wouldn't normally. You have a strong work ethic. Everyone thinks highly of you, which is probably what makes this even more uncomfortable.*

Noor: *Thank you. My work means a lot to me.*

Kim: *I'd like to explore what you can do and select resources so your private life doesn't cascade into your professional life. We'll focus on the support for things that impact work. Resources other than me. Another option is to co-develop some goals to help you continue your excellent work. Personal issues can interfere with work, muddy things up. I know you know the difference between your personal and professional lives. I'm bringing this up because, as your supervisor, I'm concerned. What do think about what I've said so far?*

Noor: *I agree. I know this. That's what doubles my embarrassment.*

Kim: *Yes. It seems learning and embarrassment are a strange couple. I also wonder if your level of education makes this more difficult.*

Noor: *[chuckle]. It does, but it will pass. Let's keep going.*

Kim: *Okay. I have three concerns, the third we can easily tweak… (objective, changeable behaviors compared against a standard).*

[later]

Kim: *You sounded like a "scientist" a minute ago, solving a problem. What's the first step?*

Noor: *First, no more late arrivals or reschedules. Second, I'll contact HR.*

Kim: *That sounds good. Remember family can participate in EAP. HR is your go-to for that. I won't be any help. A thought about that tweakable third concern – time away, a Monday or a Friday off. I actually want the team to start scheduling it instead of calling in.*

Noor: *That's a good idea. I tend to put off real vacation time.*

Kim: *Self-care. My sup sometimes has to remind me. Okay, let's create three goals…*

HOW: The following can facilitate a clinical supervision discussion on performance issues exacerbated by personal difficulties.

1. Document, document, document. Supervisor and supervisee sign each document. Keep your own journal notebook.

2. Discuss how personal issues, even among the most professional, can subtly impact work performance via examples unique to the supervisee.

3. Help the supervisee "see" the relationship between personal difficulties and work-related problems, if not already evident to the supervisee. An explicit, but sensitive, focus on how personal issues influence clinical performance prevents the supervisor from drifting into a "therapist" role. This can include Noor's professional "embarrassment" or how changes in her behavior made clients concerned about her welfare.

4. To better resolve concerns, clarify them objectively, measurably.

5. Co-develop SMART supervisee goals that include the necessary steps to improve performance, minimize confusion, and enhance success. Discuss EAP (strictly between supervisee and HR and not a part of goals). Explore starting the clinical day an hour later and leaving an hour later, use of scheduled paid time away, or other options that can support the supervisee's resolution of personal issues that impact performance.

CLINICAL SUPERVISION DOCUMENTATION

Immediate, thorough, and SMART documentation of each supervision session facilitates several dimensions of clinical supervision.

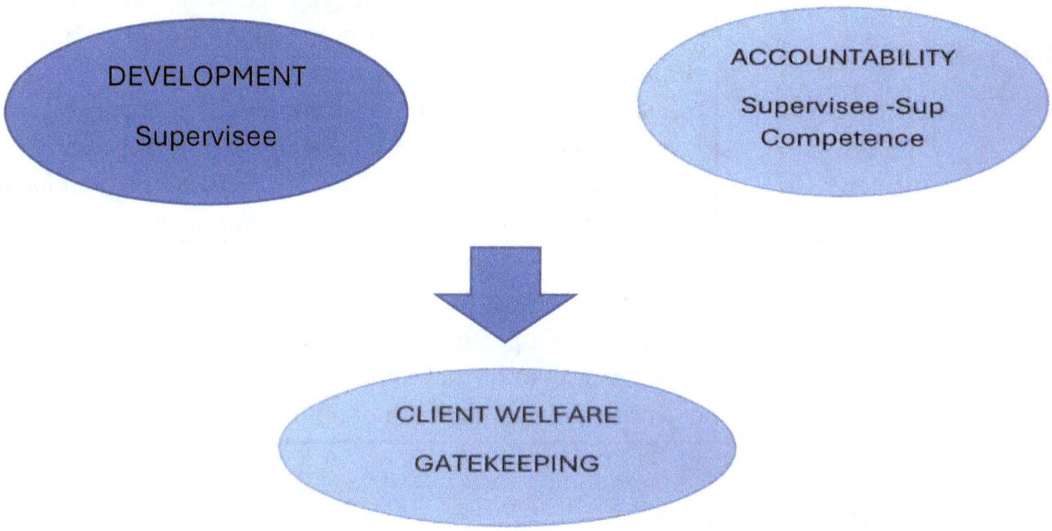

(below should be sufficiently clear for an external audit)

IMPORTANCE	DESCRIBED
Supervision sessions	Frequency and rationale
Content and outcome of each concern	Formative/summative feedback on work samples alongside a copy of the standard --Client progress reviews (risk management) --Supervisee goal reviews and updates
Due process for supervisee and supervisor	Signatures on each session note stipulate --Content and outcome authenticity --Understanding of, agreement with content and outcome
	Supervision Log, annual evaluation, remediation plan are used by the supervisor, administration, and HR for performance appraisals and merit pay increases. Important to note that they're **admissible in court proceedings.** Legally, SMART feedback and goal development increases rigor of supervisor decisions and eliminates subjectivity so change. EX: Supervisee explored countertransference. Supervisee actively reviewed specific session and developed 2 goals specific to it (*focus on clinical practice, not personal information or opinion that could fall under the private or confidential category*).
	Those related to clients are separate from standard supervisory documents. One is for client care (confidential), the other for supervisee competence. HR can access standard supervision notes in cases of formal complaints or remediation. Focus is on objective clinical practice, not opinion.

Time and Supervision

Most practitioners need either one hour weekly – not independently licensed - or one hour monthly supervision – independently licensed. The typical supervisee caseload for a supervisor is seven (7), although I've had more *as a seasoned supervisor.*

Hmm? I thought I heard … I thought you asked where you'd find the time. I'll tell you, although you won't like it. Unless you prefer to be a mediocre or poor supervisor, there are two ways to make this work:

1. Invest time front-loading your process so it will run itself indefinitely.

2. Load your process constantly and blame it on "how busy I am."

Look, I'm neither brilliant nor am I a spring chicken. If I can do this, anyone can. The problem is most simply choose not to and complain regularly. Inertia is tough to overcome and our lizard brain can make us feel good about maintaining it to save energy in the moment. Luckily for me, those who choose the second more difficult option know not to complain to me.

TIME MGMT HINT	DESCRIBED
Collaborate with other supervisors	A shared load is lighter load
Plan everything in writing	Gather data. Notice what's already in place. Create steps for what isn't. For example, most supervisors already have supervision scheduled. Do you have the contract and informed consent? Write the steps.
Feedback is addictive	Supervisees, if you deliver feedback well, will solicit it.
Supervision modality	1:1, triadic, group, peer, ... Know what to use the modality for. 1:1 is not for hard-to-hear feedback.
Individual or 1:1	One supervisor with one supervisee is the standard in supervision. Not surprisingly, it's labor and time-intensive. Many disciplines have rigorous requirements for only this modality and often from supervisors of the same discipline as the supervisee.
Triadic	One supervisor with two supervisees. Some agencies use the model that relies on three supervisees who rotate the supervisee, observer, and supervisor each session. The level of feedback will be monitored to spare feelings. This method is frequently used during graduate study field experiences, where constructive feedback is provided privately.
Group	An efficient, cost-effective, low stress, more diverse format where one supervisor meets with the whole team to review cases, solicit treatment ideas, professionally develop. Supervisee-specific feedback from the supervisor is inappropriate. I've participated in groups between 6-12. The larger the group, the more vigilant the supervisor will be to draw everyone into discussions. Preplanning is required, especially supervisory sign-in sheets and logs.
Peer	Nonhierarchical and, therefore, non-evaluative. Be cautious. It's still useful because it triggers less anxiety, especially in groups and before the supervisee increases comfort with feedback. Peers who are admired for their acumen are valuable in this modality. This format is valuable especially if the peer providing feedback can engage others and is skilled in feedback delivery. If not, then they may have a different impact than hoped for. Also beware of pre-existing relationships.

TIME MGMT HINT	DESCRIBED
Other	Some clinics offer intensive supervision for supervisees who work with special or demanding populations such as personality or spectrum conditions. Often, a supervisor who specializes in the specific domain leads the group. This is in addition to the standard supervision received.

SAMPLE

SUPERVISION PROFESSIONAL DISCLOSURE STATEMENT & CONTRACT

□ Initial □ Revision

Supervisee: **Supervisor & Credentials:**

This document is a professional disclosure statement and contract between supervisee XXX and Faculty Supervisor YYY for the purpose of clinical supervision description and verification. It describes supervisory credentials and scope of competence for supervision; supervision model; confidentiality and its limitations; supervisor and supervisor responsibilities; supervisory purpose, goals, and objectives; context; evaluative methods; supervisee goals; and other variables related to the supervisory relationship that include specific language (e.g., feedback, progress, standards).

Credentials & Scope of Competence. I earned an MA .... I have over 25 years of direct client service, clinical supervision, and administrative experience and training. In addition, I have seven years of teaching experience at the university level. I am an Arizona Licensed Professional Counselor and Certified Rehabilitation Counselor. As a rehabilitation counselor, I have clinical as well as administrative experience. Clinical expertise in serving individuals with physical, intellectual, developmental, and psychiatric disabilities or concerns. My clinical practice specialty is women diagnosed with borderline personality disorder, although I am competent in the delivery of services for most adult DSM-related needs and various client groups. Administrative experience with quality assurance, auditing, and administrative supervison.

I will always alert you when a topic is outside my scope of practice. For example, I no longer serve males diagnosed with pedophilia, although I can competently supervise those who do. My preferred therapeutic modality is CBT, but the modality I implement is always based on client needs and abilities.

Supervision Model. I use a supervision model that best "fits" the supervisee, supervisee needs and abilities, and places the supervisory relationship at the core of supervision – XXX's model, which places the supervisee-supervisor relationship at the heart of supervision. It … [describe it briefly].

Confidentiality and Limits to Confidentiality

Supervision, ***in general***, is confidential except under the following circumstances:

1. Performance and comportment inside and outside clinical supervision, particularly in reference to periodic written evaluations that can include other professionals (i.e., human resources, supervisor-of-supervisor).

2. Recommendations that rely on documented supervision sessions (e.g., employment, licensure/certification).

3. Supervision formats that include other supervisees or supervisors (e.g., triadic, group, cross-supervisor supervision).

4. Ethical or standards of practice violations.

5. Legal mandate to release documents.

Purpose, Goals, Objectives

1. Monitor supervisee clinical skills and documentation to ensure client welfare gatekeeping).

2. Promote supervisee professional identity, development, and competence.

3. Fulfill supervisee licensure and/or agency licensure and accreditation requirements.

4. If supervisee is a student, fulfill field placement academic requirements.

Context

1. Minimum of one clock hour per week of group supervision (individual, triadic, hybrid).

2. Supervision location _____, on _____ (day), from ______ to ______ (time). Supervisee -- <name> -- will submit a minimum of one recording of a clinical session per week. Rescheduled appointments will occur within same week. Each week and 24 hours prior to scheduled supervison, the supervisee will either (a) email one recording of a clinical session per week + the redacted progress note related to the session (b) email an evaluation from the Site Supervisor for an observed session.

3. The following are among several methods of supervision to be used during supervision: recorded observation*, cross-supervisor observation*, role play, supervisee report, interpersonal process recall, collaborative case conceptualization

* = essential to skill development and objective feedback

4. At a minimum, each supervision session will include

a. **Review of one or more supervisee goals.** One of the essential three best practices that should occur during each supervision session and founded on the informed consent practices of supervision. When combined with feedback and reviews of client progress, reviews of 1-2 goal reviews each session facilitate the dyad's review and reprioritization of supervisee SMART goals (i.e., specific, observable/measurable, attainable, realistic to developmental stage and needs, time-limited). Goal foci include the therapeutic alliance and outcomes, competence, and professional development.

b. **Feedback based on concrete work samples.** One of the essential three best practices, feedback during each supervision session is the cornerstone of supervisee professional development. It is a bidirectional and non-dichotomous process intended to stimulate supervisee self-assessment in the short-term and self-supervision in the long-term. Moreover, it serves as a tool for assessing the effectiveness of delivered supervision. Feedback is articulated as a statement, not a question. When limited to three constructive statements and balanced with praise, it allows supervisees to compare their work to clinical standards and agency expectations. To result in meaningful change, feedback is timely, specific, and based on observable and changeable supervisee behaviors not supervisee self-report or supervisor personal opinion. Supervisors can draw work samples from a range of formats, settings, and treatment phases. Included are direct observations or recordings of client sessions (e.g., individual, group) with multiple diagnoses or issues, client outcomes, and documentation reviews. Equally as important, continuous feedback can defuse the anxiety often associated with traditional formal summative evaluation (e.g., performance review), when supervisees are required to meet minimum standards to continue employment.

c. **Client progress reviews**: One of the essential three best practices during each supervision session. One or two systematic client progress reviews, in combination with data-based feedback, allow supervisors to assess whether and how client needs are met as well as supervisee learning needs. The reviews meet supervisory ethical-legal obligations while they contribute to timely and informed decision-making, particularly during early supervisee development.

Evaluative Methods

1. Data-informed feedback (i.e., observation/recording, documentation) will be provided each supervision session. While reviews of progress will occur on an ongoing basis, they will occur formally at mid-term and last week of term.

2. The supervisee will evaluate the supervisor after each supervision session. At a minimum, feedback to supervisor will occur at least monthly.

3. Supervision session logs will be completed and signed by supervisee and Faculty Supervisor before end of same day supervision occurs. Supervisee will retain a copy.

Terms

ACES supervisory best practices & Ethics Code (* = each supervision session)

1. Initiate supervision
2. Supervisee goal-setting*
3. Provide feedback*
4. Client progress reviews*
5. Supervisory relationship health
6. Diversity and advocacy considerations
7. Ethical considerations

8. Documentation

9. Evaluation

10. Supervision format

11. The supervisor: competent, ethical, balanced

12. Supervisor preparation (training and supervision of supervision)

Competence, effectiveness, satisfaction triad: Competence is conferred by laws and best practices, and specifies the basic skills required to perform a specific task. Effectiveness is the objective degree to which a task's desired outcomes are achieved. Satisfaction is the subjective rating on the outcome of a specific task. Competence need not result in effectiveness or satisfaction. A supervisor may demonstrate the requisite range of skills and still not achieve desired outcomes or supervisee satisfaction. Conversely, supervisees may be satisfied with a supervisor who knows, but does not demonstrate the requisite range of knowledge and skills.

Supervisory Relationship: The dyadic relationship resides at the heart of productive supervision, influences supervisee competence and professional growth, and client welfare. The supervisory relationship is essential for meeting client welfare and gatekeeping practices. The supervisor's evaluative and expert powers are derived directly from those obligations to clients. Since the supervisor has the primary responsibility for the relationship, some essential supervisor traits include self-awareness, dependable and ethical conduct, warm authority, strong administrative and clinical skills, and cultural sensitivity.

Gatekeeping: The ethical and legal obligation that ensures practitioners unsuited for the practice in word, deed, attitude are restricted from the counseling profession. This is based strictly on data, not opinion.

Supervisee will ...

1. Immediately alert Site Supervisor of crises or incidents. If the Site Supervisor cannot be reached, the supervisee will contact the Faculty Supervisor (XXX-YYY-ZZZZ).

2. Follow Site Supervisor directions as provided. In order to do that, the supervisee will ensure full understanding of directions.

3. Prepare for and attend individual/triadic site and academic supervision sessions as scheduled. Cancel/reschedule will occur a minimum of 24 hours in advance.
4. Submit weekly recording or site supervisor evaluation of observed session + redacted note. The supervisee will review that recorded session prior to supervision in order to identify specific section(s) that highlight strengths and need for support.
5. Be prepared to discuss progress of any of assigned clients during supervision.
6. Be prepared to discuss and modify professional goals.
7. Solicit and be open to feedback that is supported with samples of supervisee work and samples of the desired standard.
8. Justify client case conceptualizations, approaches, and techniques used.
9. Complete all client-related documentation within 24 clock hours.
10. Implement supervisory feedback or directives according to the timeline provided. If none is provided, supervisee will ask.
11. Increase competence with multiple therapeutic modalities to meet diverse client needs.
12. Maintain a one-million-dollar liability policy at all times if supervisee is a student or works in a private practice.
13. Maintain a supervision notebook that includes supervision goals, supervision session notes, and hours.
14. Practice self-care to minimize impairment.
15. Provide direct feedback to supervisor after each supervision session.

Supervisor will...

1. Be available Monday through Friday between 8AM and 6PM with precise, clear, and direct guidance.

2. Prepare for and attend supervision sessions as scheduled. Cancel/reschedule will occur with a minimum of 24-hour advance notice. Make-up supervision will occur in the same week.
3. Not abuse supervisory authority.
4. Review samples of assessments, service plans, and service-related documentation to ensure cohesiveness between all three.
5. Directly observe or review at least one supervisee clinical recording per week.
6. Provide clear and balanced feedback each supervision session based on concrete samples of supervisee work, not supervisor "opinion". This includes periodic formal written evaluations, and corrective plans as indicated by supervisee progress. All feedback is supported with samples of supervisee work and standard(s) on which it is based and is congruent with supervisee phase of development.
7. Review supervisee goals, and modify goals based on progress.
8. Review and sign field placement documents.
9. Challenge supervisee to justify clinical approach and techniques used to enhance self-awareness, case conceptualization skills, and increase knowledge of various therapeutic approaches.
10. Intervene when client welfare is at risk.
11. Intervene when supervisee welfare is at risk.
12. Model and discuss ethical behavior according to professional standards.
13. Model and discuss culturally ethical behavior.
14. Maintain and secure supervision notes.
15. Provide learning opportunities about supervision and a an opportunity to supervise.

Supervisee Goals

--MANDATORY: Concise clinical documentation

Separate notation for every client and client-related interaction – therapy, case management, case consultation

--MANDATORY: Clinical documentation linked to SMART service plan

--X

--X

Concerns. I adhere to the codes of professional conduct outlined by the Arizona Board of Behavioral Health Examiners, the American Counseling Association, and Commission on Rehabilitation Counselor Certification. I hope you will discuss concerns with me first. Otherwise, contact the Counseling Program Director – Dr. Amanda Tashjian (email, phone).

Terms of the Contract. The supervisor reserves the right to terminate clinical supervision should the supervisee be unable or unwilling to adhere to a corrective wellness plan related to impairment.

This contract is subject to revision at any time as requested by supervisee or supervisor. Both supervisee and supervisor will approve revisions.

Supervisee and supervisor collaborated on the development of this contract. Both agree to uphold the directives specified in this supervision contract and do so according to professional ethical principles.

SAMPLE

CLINICAL SUPERVISION LOG

Date: **Duration:**

Supervisee: **Type**: 1:1 **Mode**: In-Person, Zoom, Telephone

Abbreviations

aeb = as evidenced by, b/c = because, bro/sis = brother/sister, bx = behavior, client = client, CM = Case Mgr, d = day, DTS/O = danger to self/ others, esp = especially, ETOH = alcohol, FB = feedback, HI/SI = homicidal/suicidal ideation, ISP = individual service plan, LTG/ STG = long-term/short-term goal, MI = motivational interviewing, MSE = mental status exam, prac = practicum, prn = as needed, PSG = parasuicidal gesture, q = every, rcv = receive, s.o. = significant other, sup = supervisor, supee = supervisee, sx = symptom, tx = treatment, w/o = without, WSL = within standard limits

Supervisee Presentation: Sup completes

Client Review of Progress: Supee completes

Data-based FB re service delivery, documentation, etc.: Supee completes

Supee professional goals: Supee completes

1. Recording brought to every session, reviewed a minimum of every third session

Supervisee Tasks by Next Supervision Session

1. If content is accurate, supee signs PDF Clinical Supervision Log, returns to Sup by end of same day
2. Minimum 24 hours prior to 1:1 Supervision > 1 session recording + redacted clinical note + redacted ISP

Supervisor Tasks by Next Supervision Session

1. Complete & convert Supervision Log to PDF, sign, email to supee for approval
2.

My signature below attests to the accuracy of this Clinical Supervision Log.

CONCLUDING THOUGHTS

This is the end.

A friend asked me what I hoped to achieve with this. I replied I needed to think.

I work with the best – Marcela Kepic, Sue Kroeger, Brian Clarke, Mike Hartley, Elissa Munoz, Jina Yoon, Liz Pina, and Vanessa Perry who left to be a physician's assistant. No two alike. Perfect. None works harder than a committed professor and researcher. Please let me have this one. We produce counselors -- no easy task. Hands on, all the time. Then, there are the forms, data tracking, service.... The bottom line is I said yes to this profession and, no matter how tired I am, I keep going. I'm tired but alive. The individuals above are much like me.

But the world has changed. Not changed as in I'm a grumpy old woman who no longer clicks in tandem with the world. I click; I tandem.

Anyway, to respond to that question at the top of the page: I did this because this new world is going to need more counselors with exquisite skills. So, help us build a clinic.

www.ingramcontent.com/pod-product-compliance
Lightning Source LLC
LaVergne TN
LVHW080047210926
848481LV00011B/3291
9798385186327